MARRIED AND LONELY

A Dynamic, Interactive Workbook for Singles and Couples

Pastor R. D. Bernard

iUniverse books may be ordered through booksellers or by contacting:

iUniverse
1663 Liberty Drive
Bloomington, IN 47403
www.iuniverse.com
1-800-Authors (1-800-288-4677)

Because of the dynamic nature of the Internet, any web addresses or links contained in this book may have changed since publication and may no longer be valid. The views expressed in this work are solely those of the author and do not necessarily reflect the views of the publisher, and the publisher hereby disclaims any responsibility for them.

Any people depicted in stock imagery provided by Thinkstock are models, and such images are being used for illustrative purposes only.
Certain stock imagery © Thinkstock.

ISBN: 978-1-5320-0490-2 (sc)
ISBN: 978-1-5320-0491-9 (e)

Print information available on the last page.

iUniverse rev. date: 09/09/2016

Contents

Prologue

The idea for "Married and Lonely" came from years of pastoral study and discussion as it relates to marriage, singleness, spirituality, and relationships of all kinds. Although the Case Studies contain names, dates, places, and events that are fictional, the stories that they tell and the underlying themes are universal in nature. Any similarity to any person living or dead is purely coincidental and merely reflects the collective nature of the life that we all live. My story is contained within these pages, as well as your story and the stories of countless others.

While "Married and Lonely" is meant to be a self-help workbook for singles and couples, it is not meant to be a "cure-all." It definitely is not a "how-to" book. It is simply meant to help us see ourselves – whether we are single, married, divorced, or widowed – and point the way forward.

"Married and Lonely" is to be read as a progressive work. The lessons build one lesson upon the next. The contents of each Case Study provide lively examples for discussion.

Lesson #1 begins with "Addressing the Elephant in the Room." This lesson is about how most marriages end up lonely: two single people who placed sex, "the elephant in the room," at the center of their marriage. It details how, in certain people's minds, if what is going on in the bed is not right, then the whole marriage is not right.

This lesson also discusses how sexual sicknesses follow us throughout life. The Case Study, "It's All out in the Open," is a realistic example of the infidelity present in many marriages and what the root causes are.

Lesson #2, "The Little Things," argues that it's the little things that destroy relationships. The "little things" are those values (e.g., truth, trust, caring, love, etc.) that are so fundamental to marriage that the marriage can't function without them. These values are not present if Christ is not at the center of the relationship.

The Case Study example of Dr. and Mrs. Loving and Illustration 2-1, demonstrate how even the most dedicated and spiritual marriages may cease to be satisfying over the years because of the neglect of the little things.

Lesson #3, "Busy Days and Lonely Nights," discusses the different forms of loneliness and how they impact relationships. This lesson also discusses various ways to share your "tender grapes" with your partner. The Case Study, "Sophie's Soul Searching," is an extended example of a woman who has struggled with loneliness for most of her life.

Lesson #4, "The History of Your Heart," is foundational to any good relationship. This lesson discusses the effect of past relationships on present relationships. This portion of the book gives examples of the many emotional hindrances that can be present in one's heart and how to release these past sins and hurts.

The Case Study to this lesson, "Ruthie's Dilemma," pertains to a young lady who is new to the Faith, who has to deal with some old baggage.

Of course, one of the prerequisites for marriage is eligible single people, so Lesson #5, "Singleness Matters," discusses the role and purpose of "singleness" in the lives of believers. It demonstrates how a life lived with integrity as a single person is the starting point to a strong marriage.

The Case Study in this lesson and Illustrations 5-1 and 5-2, are meant to be comprehensive examples of how our experiences as single people feed into our marriages. The examples of Jane and John, our fictional wife and husband, will be referred to throughout the lessons. Their life experiences are presented pictorially in Illustrations 5-1and 5-2, respectively.

Lesson #6, "Seasoned and Satisfied," focuses on some of the more common issues faced by seniors as they age in marriage. This lesson also points out the pitfalls of marriages entered into later in life. The example of Elijah and Sarah in the Case Study could be any one of a number of seasoned saints who married late in life.

Of course if all "self-help" fails, Lesson #7 discusses "Professional Help." Couples need to know when to ask for help and how prolonged living without help can ruin our patterns of thinking as it pertains to relationships.

Illustration 7-1 and the Case Study, Jim and Kate Stringer, "It's Hard!" detail how overwhelming life can be. Our relationships exist within a world of obligations and responsibilities. These obligations and responsibilities can drive us to the brink of disaster if we don't know when to seek professional help.

"Know Thyself," reads the ancient Greek aphorism. It is my belief that as we are led and guided toward self-awareness, the more open we become to God's healing and the Holy Spirit's leading. Only then can we find our place and our peace in this world.

As a minister of the Gospel, much of what is presented within these pages is presented from a Biblical perspective. I do not argue for the truth of Scripture in this volume, the truth is self-evident.

"Married and Lonely" is an excellent study aid/discussion guide in both singles and marriage groups and workshops. Its teachings are universal and cover all facets of life and relationships.

Like any author, I am indebted to so many whose lives and work have enriched mine. Thank you to the officers, members and friends of the King Solomon Baptist Church of Vicksburg, Mississippi, who have allowed the Word of God to have free course. I am especially grateful to my Administrative Assistant, Linda Sandles, who has always provided invaluable assistance.

I am also indebted to the many family members and friends who faithfully read draft after draft of this volume. Thank you all for providing your reasoned and candid feedback.

Last, but certainly not least, thank you to my loving wife, Valerie, and our two dutiful sons, David and Daniel. They have allowed me the spiritual space to serve others, to serve them, and to make myself more useful to the Kingdom of God.

Pastor R.D. Bernard
Vicksburg, Mississippi
October 2016

Preface

"All night long on my bed, I looked for the one my heart loves. I looked for him but did not find him." Song of Solomon 3:1

You walk in the house after a hard day's work or a busy day of running around town. You see your loved one. You know that you love them, but there is no affection between the two of you.

You want to reach out and hold them, but you don't know how to or whether your affection will even be returned. So you retreat yet again into the cold formality of a marriage without intimacy.

Perhaps you both speak, maybe even smile, but you continue with your routine and your spouse with theirs. You know that you love one another, but maybe, and this is a BIG maybe, you are no longer "in love" with one another.

The dinner is ready. The house is clean, or clean enough. The children are healthy or are grown and gone. Your heart wants some "us" time or just some meaningful conversation for a change. As you prepare for dinner or your evening routine, you know that you will not get any "us" time, yet again tonight.

You feel trapped in a relationship that *used* to work. You have a lot of life left to live, but without relational intimacy, you really feel like you are dying a slow, suffocating death.

You have arrived. You are officially one of the millions of Americans who is married and lonely. You have plenty of activity in your life, but what you could use a lot more of is intimacy. You want to be understood. You want to be close physically to someone else. You want to feel desired and loved.

Maybe you just want to talk. You still have lots of hopes, fears, and dreams. Sometimes, you just want someone to listen while you talk about what happened that particular day! Yes, your heart desires companionship.

Divorce is not an option, yet. Although you may not stray, your mind and imagination do. You wonder what it would be like to have this intimacy and companionship with someone else. You remember how magical it was in the early days with your spouse.

Your dreams are invaded by thoughts and images from those days. Sometimes you feel that if the right person said the right thing on the right day, well let's just be thankful that hasn't happened. Still, how do you deal with being married and lonely?

It all begins with "Addressing the Elephant in the Room."

Lesson #1

"Addressing the Elephant in the Room"

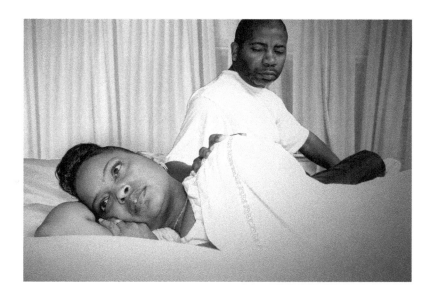

"Do not arouse or awaken my love before the time." Song of Solomon 8:4

If it's not right in the marriage bed, it's usually not right at all. We live in the midst of a sex-saturated, sex-crazed, and, mostly, sexually-sick society. Yes, sexuality is a most satisfying part of our existence. Let's face reality. When the sex is not right, *we* are not right. When *we* are not right, the marriage or the relationship is *definitely* not right.

There, the Pastor wrote it; I addressed the elephant in the room. Sex is the proverbial "elephant in the room" that must be *truly* addressed by each of us in our relationships. The elephant is not the room, but it sure does take up a lot of space in the room. Sex means that much to most people – married and single.

Understanding this elephant may be the key to avoiding some of the more common pitfalls in relationships. To borrow Solomon's thoughts in Song of Solomon 8:4, the power of our sexuality is awakened way too early.

Sex is Power!

Sex, outside of the covenant relationship of marriage, is pure power! When awakened too early, it has resulted in life-long addictive and compulsive behaviors. For instance, some men only view women in sexual terms – they see the elephant and not the person. They want to know: *"How does she look?"* Translation: *"Is she fine?"*

In a similar manner, many women know the power of sex, especially that of the uncommitted variety. Some don't feel themselves to be loved by a man, or even in a real relationship, unless there is sex. When there is no sex, women doubt themselves: *"Am I desirable?"* They may even doubt the sexuality of the man: *"Is he gay?"* In these cases, the elephant *always* becomes the center of the relationship.

How many of us truly understand sex? How many of us understand its raw power when untamed by a spiritual covenant? Sex sells everything from beauty products to clothes, to cars, to homes, and probably ice to Eskimos. Sex has been the cause of much death and carnage throughout the ages, not to mention innumerable nasty divorces and breakups.

It is worth it to attempt a deeper understanding of this elephant, and how it affects our relationships. Sex is not just physical. It is also not just mental. Whether we realize it or not, this is one act that we perform with the totality of our being.

The mental, emotional, and spiritual content of each of us is laid bare during the physical act of intercourse. Whatever we are, or have been as total persons is cumulatively present during the act of intercourse. That's right. We bring our whole psycho-sexual histories each time we participate in this one act.

Again, sex is not the mere physical act that most perceive it as being. The physical act of intercourse is a coming together of two as "one flesh." The manner, the means, the biology, and the anatomy of this act touches the realm of the sacred – whether one is married or not.

God made us to desire. When performed within the covenant relationship of marriage, sex is an act of spiritual worship. The marriage partners are called by God to come together, regularly, in this joyful union.

> **Try This**
>
> ✓ **For each time that you "fellowship," schedule another time just to hold one another and talk.**

It is a symbol of the two formerly separate lives and life directions which have now been brought together into one life pattern and direction for His glory. In marriage, the "fellowship" in the bedroom (and wherever else) should be excellent!

Yet this "excellent act" should occur as the *culmination* of the union of husband and wife. To build a relationship on sex is to give the elephant center stage. What passes for passion in a platonic relationship should be based on personality, not sex. Of course, the majority of us have aroused or awakened sexual love before the time.

This casual sex, or "friends with benefits," continues sometimes even when the "relationship" is over. Even in these relationships, the power of the sexual act is still there. The act of worship is also there. However, the object of worship or adoration is not God; it is to the elephant itself.

Sex on Demand

Did I mention that very few understand the power of sex? The Apostle Paul called the union of husband and wife a "mystery." The one-ness of their "one-flesh" union has its origins and likenesses in the very persons of the Godhead.

This powerful, spiritual union has the potential to disintegrate into sex-on-demand, especially in marriage. Marriage partners, and let's not kid ourselves, even potential marriage partners, are expected to have a sexual "sizzle" about them. This is what some call "love," "sex-appeal," or just plain "chemistry." It's also what wives are expected to have to keep their husbands happy and at home. Husbands, as well, are expected to "perform" with their "penis power," so that wives will remain "in love" with them.

The trouble at home usually begins when one partner turns his or her back on the other partner in the marriage bed one time too many. Sex, without true commitment, is power, and it is quite common for spouses to attempt to punish one another through what does or does not happen in the marriage bed.

Sexual Sickness

Of course, trouble in the marriage bed can also arise from any one of a number of factors, some trivial: *"You stared at her just a little too long,"* or *"You sure were smiling an awful lot when he spoke to you."*

Exclusivity in sex, doesn't mean that there aren't any problems. When there is any type of emotional sickness anywhere in the life of one who is a party to this "one-flesh" arrangement, it will be felt in the marriage bed, even if not spoken.

Unresolved resentment, bitterness, anger, un-forgiveness, jealousy, malice, deceit and other strong emotions from years past are all still present in our emotional lives. These will ultimately reverberate throughout the marriage, including the marriage bed. Remember, marriage is a spiritual union, and sex is sacred. Deep-seated problems in marriage may seem to revolve around sex; however, these problems existed before the marriage.

Sex is not the problem, we are. As you will learn in Lesson #4, our hearts have histories. These emotional histories do continue to manifest from time to time. When our "fellowship" in the bedroom becomes imperfect or even irregular, there is a hidden problem whose symptoms are now in the open, begging for a cure.

Sexual issues with a partner, or with sex itself, usually don't concern the present partner at all, especially if you have not been married for a number of years.

For relationships that do not have long, long, committed histories, the issue is usually due to an unresolved past event that is still manifesting in the present. The issue could have as its origin, something that happened when a person was single, as we discuss in Lesson #5, "Singleness Matters," or the issue could be even farther back.

Awakening Your Sexual Being

Consider how and when a person awakens his or her sexuality. Sexually, what a person practices early enough and frequently enough, is what he or she defines as "normal." "Normal" is then the expectation level, even if it is truly "abnormal."

Most have aroused or awakened the elephant in the room long before the time, and often in ways that were less than ideal, such as incest, molestation, sodomy, rape, or other forms of sexual abuse. Of course, statistics would also validate the fact that very few men and women allow their relationships to culminate in married sex.

Likewise, psychologists, psychotherapists, and other mental health professionals are still measuring the negative effects of pornography, masturbation, and other "self-satisfying" sexual acts whether a person is single or married.

All of these sexual practices and "prior instances" will show up in the marriage bed. You may be in a relationship with one person, but the marriage bed is really full of people. Can you hear the unspoken thoughts of your partner or maybe even your own? *"Where did she learn this?" "Who else has he shared himself with?"*

Try This
....

✓ **Pray at the foot of the marriage bed before "fellowshipping."**

Of course, there are also certain "requirements" that some partners have in the marriage bed. These are the "non-negotiables" that many younger people insist are mandatory. These "requirements" seem to satisfy one partner, while denigrating and otherwise denying the personhood of their spouse. In essence, this is one person exercising his or her power over the other, without regard to the God-given sanctity of married, monogamous sex. This is the old, *"my wife is my property,"* argument.

We don't fully understand the damage we have done to others, in the name of love, through insisting on having our way in the marriage bed or even before we ever make it to the marriage bed. How many of our former partners who are now married to others, are still carrying the emotional issues with which we scarred them?

Bad Boy and Bad Girl Sex

When sex is awakened in a manner than is unbecoming of an act of worship performed in covenant relationship, compulsive behaviors are birthed. These behaviors, usually exhibited outside the bedroom, deny our ultimate fulfillment as spiritual beings, in the bedroom and elsewhere.

For example, the feelings of abandonment, worthlessness, emptiness, loneliness, and meaninglessness that accompany some relationships are good signposts that we have unresolved issues deep in our hearts. Each successive sexual partner and each sexual act then becomes an exercise in futility. It is always the other person's fault, or so we think.

The Battle for Center Stage

We are the "what's in it for me?" and the "can-do" generation. "How-to" books for the bedroom, DVDs, movies, or any other form of "sex-aid," will not suffice for what *truly* ails relationships.

Indeed, it doesn't matter whether one is over-sexed or under-sexed, if your starting point was wrong, the foundation for the relationship is wrong. The elephant is indeed there, attempting to take center stage, but center stage was not made for the elephant; it was made for the Lion.

"And one of the elders said unto me, 'Weep not: behold, the Lion of the tribe of Judah, the Root of David, hath prevailed...'" Revelation 5:5. As we will find out in Lesson #2, without the Lion, the elephant is just a one-act show.

Case Study – Lesson #1

"Addressing the Elephant in the Room"

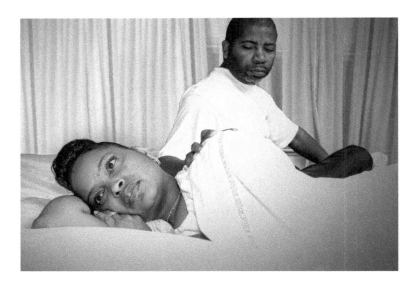

"Do not arouse or awaken my love before the time." Song of Solomon 8:4

Ron and Sandra Robinson – "It's All out in the Open"

"You said we needed professional help, now I'm here!" Ron shouted. "I didn't want to be here. I'm here because of you!"

"You should be here because of *us*!" his wife, Sandra, returned his shout. "We have a home and a son, *together!*" The couple, now standing, was nearly face to face, neither backing down.

In any other setting, this exchange may have ended with one or both of the partners storming off. But this was a controlled setting –the office of their marriage counselor, Dr. Brandon Smith.

Dr. Smith gave Ron and Sandra Robinson great latitude in this session. He knew what the issues were, but his professional ethics forbade him from speaking plainly. The husband and wife must bring everything out in the open, themselves. During the last six sessions, they had only made spotty progress, at best.

The sole issue that had been conceded is that the level of intimacy in their marriage had changed. Sandra practically shouted it every chance she got. "Dr. Smith, he won't even *touch* me. He acts like he doesn't want to come home at night, and when he does get home, if he comes to bed at all, he turns his back to me. What kind of a man regularly does that? Ron has never been this way, not even when we were dating. For Ron to go a week or two without touching me and not be sick, he has got to be seeing somebody else."

The tears rolled slowly down Sandra's face. It wasn't the cascade of tears that Dr. Smith had come to expect from previous sessions. Sandra was getting past crying. The normally demure wife, mother, and elementary school teacher, was slowly getting angry. The only reason she suggested counseling in the first place was to get Ron to admit that he was being unfaithful. There were many days and nights that she thought, "*If Ron would just acknowledge his infidelity, we could get past this.*"

For his part, Ron would only listen and stare blankly at his wife of six years. Things *had* changed. Sandra was no longer the woman that he just "had to have." She just didn't stimulate him like she used to. When he looked at her, he saw Ron Jr.'s mother and the task-master who ran his house, not a lover. True, she had aged, but they were both only thirty-seven.

In recent months, they had the occasional tryst in the marriage bed, but those were just "bumps in the night," more convenience than anything else. In years past, they actually seemed to *live*. They didn't have self-imposed curfews and money was no issue. Hadn't he always told her that he didn't "live to work"?

Ron's job paid plenty, but Sandra seemed to need more and more. When Ron didn't have it, or refused to pay for what he considered "wants," the accusing started. Ron felt bad enough having to balance the responsibility of being a husband and father, with also trying to have a little enjoyment in life. In one of the sessions, Ron had the realization that Sandra had been accusing him long before he started seeing someone else secretly.

Ron was not the reflective type, so he never really wondered what happened to his marriage. Sure, there was the responsibility of the house and their son, Ron Jr., but everything now seemed so serious to Sandra.

In previous sessions, when confronted by Sandra about possible infidelity, Ron would vehemently deny it, and then proceed to talk about her nit-picking and fault-finding. "Doc, any way that she can steal my happiness, she will do it. I can't have an occasional cold beer with friends or just be alone away from home, without her accusing me. She checks my car, my phone, and my wallet. She complains about me not being at home, but what man can put up with this?" Then, he looked directly at Sandra and said, "Where is the trust?"

He knew she had no proof. Sandra was actually *too* trusting. Ron wasn't ready for a divorce. He still loved Sandra in his own way. He just wasn't "in love" with her. He once was, but the accusing seemed to kill whatever love was left. There was no way he was going to admit to any infidelity and give her the satisfaction of being right.

Life was so serious all of a sudden. Ron didn't think much past today or tomorrow. In his own mind, he was just "trying to make it." At least he was there, in the home with his child. Some men couldn't say that. Sandra helped pay bills and provide a home for Ron Jr., whom he loved dearly, but it was Rebecca who made Ron feel like a real man.

Of course, Rebecca was the elephant in the room. No one conceded her existence except Sandra. Sandra couldn't name her, or place her in Ron's life in any concrete way, but she knew that another woman was indeed there. She could feel it!

Sandra was in such emotional turmoil. She *knew* Ron had someone else, but as long as he stayed quiet about it and was careful, she had no proof. On more than one occasion Ron had asked her, "Why can't you accept the fact that I am at home with you and Ron, Jr.? *You are my wife.*"

"And she is your *tramp*," Sandra said quietly just this morning when they were on their way to the Counselor's office, "I will not give up on my marriage."

Proof or not, Sandra was determined not to be like many of the younger teachers at her school, who turned blind eyes and deaf ears to infidelity. It seemed to be a way of life in this community. Everybody did it, and it was okay, as long as everyone was discreet.

It was once that way with Sandra as well, but now she wanted to make God a part of her life. Years ago, she and Ron's pastor told them that a relationship with God "means being out in the open about everything."

So Sandra refused to be married and lonely. She wouldn't settle for just "saddling up with Ron" once a month in the middle of the night, when they were both half-asleep. She wanted Ron to need her just as she needed him. Sure, she would have been considered a "loose" woman at the time that she met Ron, but their marriage had changed all of that.

Sandra was determined to be a good wife. She had already failed at marriage once, and so had Ron. Their previous marriages ended along the same lines that threatened this one – infidelity and the inability to address it.

"Ron, why the big change in your life?" asked Dr. Smith. Dr. Smith knew full well that Ron had at least one mistress. Did Ron really think that he was fooling anybody? The counseling was at a standstill because Ron refused to be truthful. Dr. Smith was very careful about how he approached this one issue. It was okay for Sandra to say it, but if Dr. Smith openly agreed, Ron would probably leave and never come back.

When confronted with his bizarre behavior, Ron would just reply, "I don't know. I guess I am tired. When I get home…"

"Sometimes you don't even come home," Sandra interrupted.

Ron looked directly at Dr. Smith and then continued. "Well, *Doctor*, when I *do* come home, I get very little support from my wife."

Ron wondered privately how he ever felt about Sandra the way he now felt about Rebecca, or his 'Becke,' as he playfully called her. Becke was forty-something, but she made Ron feel like he was twenty all over again!

Although Becke knew he was married, she was always eager to make Ron feel like a man. Men had large appetites, and Ron, seemingly, could not get enough. This was something he never got from Sandra, at least not lately.

How would he ever be able to tell his wife something like this? He didn't think he could do it, even if he tried. *What's the use anyway,* he thought. It just seemed easier not to mention anything – everybody should just go along and try to get along. Wouldn't discussing it needlessly hurt a lot of people?

But Sandra, in her newfound anger, insisted on calling their situation 'the elephant in the room.' Every now and then she would text Ron little things like, "Are you coming home to eat, or are you eating wherever you are?" or "Are you coming home tonight, or does the elephant have you preoccupied?"

Sandra was always trying to fix him, he thought. Didn't she know that women couldn't fix men? She even took him back to church. Ron knew that what was happening in his life was *way* deeper than church.

If the preacher was a real man, then he should understand men. Men have been doing this for ages. Ron had been busy at it since he was 15. Certainly, the Reverend could give him an "A-men" on that!

Now the good Dr. Smith, after months of moving slowly, wants to know why the big change in my life. Why doesn't he just come right out and ask me about the elephant in the room?

Ron knew that he would just deny it, and the counseling would be over.

QUESTIONS – LESSON #1

"ADDRESSING THE ELEPHANT IN THE ROOM"

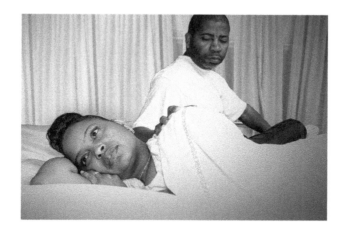

"Do not arouse or awaken my love before the time." Song of Solomon 8:4

1. How old were you and under what circumstances did you lose your virginity?

    _____

    _____

    _____

    _____

    _____

    a. Looking back, do you regret losing your virginity under those circumstances?

        _____

        _____

        _____

        _____

b. How do you believe your early sexual experiences colored your view of relationships?

_____

_____

_____

_____

2. Are you satisfied with your sex life?

_____

_____

_____

_____

_____

3. In the Case Study, how do you think Ron's early sexual experiences have distorted the way he views relationships?

_____

_____

_____

_____

_____

4. In Sandra and Ron's case, should the 'elephant in the room' (Becke) be discussed? Why or why not?

_____

_____

_____

_____

5. From the information you have been given about Ron, numerically rank the importance of the following persons, attributes, and institutions in his life, from greatest importance to least importance.

    a. God_____

    b. Becke_____

    c. Sandra_____

    d. Church_____

    e. Ron, Jr._____

    f. Sex_____

6. Can a person be addicted to sex and not know it? Why or why not?

    _____

    _____

    _____

    _____

    _____

7. Based on the information presented in Lesson #1, "Addressing the Elephant in the Room," how do you know when sex has become too important in a relationship?

    _____

    _____

    _____

    _____

    _____

8. If you were addicted to sex, would you seek professional help? Why or why not?

_____

_____

_____

_____

_____

9. Based on the information presented in Lesson #1, "Addressing the Elephant in the Room," what are some of the characteristics of sex addiction and how do they get started?

_____

_____

_____

_____

_____

10. In your opinion, does God play any role in 'addressing the elephant in the room'?

_____

_____

_____

_____

_____

Lesson #2

"The Little Things"

"Our vines have tender grapes." Song of Solomon 2:15

It is not the big things in life that wreak havoc; it is the little things. Little lies, told in the commission of the act of adultery, will destroy trust quicker than the adultery itself.

Contrary to popular opinion, little things destroy relationships. The "little things" are those values (e.g., truth, trust, caring, and love) that are so fundamental to marriage, that the marriage can't function without them.

In this day and age, it is quite difficult for people from different backgrounds and varied life experiences to come together in the 'one-flesh' arrangement of marriage.

Of course, it is wholly impossible to *truly* come together without God. God's presence ensures that the "big things" (e.g., sickness, strife, and financial hardships) can be overcome. According to Illustration 2-1, God is both the source and the direction or purpose in relationships.

Whether we are introverts or extroverts, been through a lot or been through just a little, it's difficult for us to open our hearts to other people. We reason to ourselves that since we don't quite understand ourselves and all the tough times that we have been through, it will be doubly hard exposing someone else to our imperfections.

So we put our best foot forward in relationships, while simultaneously holding back events, occurrences, or feelings about which we are particularly sensitive.

Sharing the Tender Grapes

To borrow the phraseology of Song of Solomon 2:15, we are reluctant to share our "tender grapes." The "tender grapes" represent the budding intimacy or rather the growth potential in relationships. The tender grapes both touch and expose our hearts.

When we reveal or open our hearts to others, it is the tender grapes that we are revealing. I may be expressing what is obvious; but when one has suffered through certain hardships in life, it becomes harder to share the tender grapes.

We become cold emotionally. Relationships in our lives then resemble frozen winters; no love can get in to us, and no love can get out to others. There is also an air of formality about us. No one can really get close to us – not even spouses.

The "unfortunates" of life train us to shut down in certain situations. When we shut down emotionally, usually there is no use in talking to us because we are "finished with it." *Fool me once, shame on you. Fool me twice, shame on me.*

God's Space in Your Relationship

This is where God comes in. The "Song of Solomon" has been portrayed as a symbol of a person's budding relationship with God. Sometimes, we think that we have to do all of these great and grand things to please God, but all God really wants, is for us to be faithful in the little things.

Obedience in small things brings us closer to Him. We can't control our spouses, but we can ensure that at least one spouse is controlled by God. God wants us to be intimate, first and foremost, with Him.

The strength of this most important relationship will ensure that all other relationships in our lives are healthy. It is through our closeness with Him, that we are strengthened enough to share our tender grapes with others.

The natural pre-cursor to unleashing the sacredness of sexuality is heartfelt intimacy; the place where the two become one. Yet, this heartfelt intimacy does not come naturally to any of us. Most of us are still learning how to *truly* open up to other people. Husbands are still learning to open up to wives, and wives are still learning to expose themselves, emotionally, to husbands.

Growth Means Change

Human beings are complex creations. You can never know them fully. It would surprise us all to know the true thoughts of our loved ones! We keep growing, changing, and evolving. So as we relate to one another, we have to keep on relating and growing together through all of the seasons of life.

In any relationship, the initial interface is surface level. These are the characteristics located outside the circles in Illustrations 5-1 and 5-2. These two fictitious people don't know one another's backgrounds. With God's guidance, they will learn to trust each other over the years and begin to share their tender grapes and work out the issues represented by the innermost circle.

I have been married seventeen years as of the date of publication of this book. My wife is still sharing some things with me about herself; and I am still sharing some things with her about my life prior to meeting her.

Try These Tips
✓ **Say something nice, but true, to your spouse each day.**
✓ **Pray with your spouse once daily.**

Under God's guidance, I am also learning some things about myself, that I didn't realize until I became a part of this one-flesh union. Likewise, I have been privileged to share some things with my wife concerning her, that she could not see for herself. Yes, some of these matters are painful, as you can see from the innermost circles of Illustrations 5-1 and 5-2, but they are necessary for growth.

When our loved ones share their tender grapes, it may not seem like much to us, but it is quite significant to them. All it takes is one little thing – one perceived slight – and the person who opened up will go right back into his or her shell. Like old turtles, we are trained to stick our heads out only far enough to see if it is safe.

The Importance of Tone

Relationships are so fragile that they can be destroyed by something very small – like our tones. For instance, in the home in which I grew up, there were lots of noises. There were several adults and many, many children of whom I was the youngest. My grandfather's voice could be heard booming at all the boys: "Keep quiet!" and "Play *out*side!"

Naturally, when I had boys, I "boomed" too. My tone as a new father was bad, and I didn't know it. My sons would go to their mother and ask why was I upset with them. They wanted to know what had they done.

When they were two or three years old, some of their first sentences were used to let me know that I was hurting their feelings. I knew then that we had an intimacy problem caused by a little thing, like my tone.

They would go behind chairs or in another room and cry. My tone to them said, *"I am constantly mad at y'all."* If we don't pick up on the little things, we will ruin relationships.

As a further example, a father who lives apart from his daughter may subconsciously think that he can make up for all that he didn't do during the year, by giving his daughter a "big" party for her birthday. He certainly loves his daughter; he is just busy. The party means a lot to him, but to the child, it doesn't mean very much.

Try This

....

✓ **Let the other party to the relationship define what is important to them.**

The child knows from experience that her father will not even return her calls next week. Her father is preoccupied with the size of the cake, and all his daughter is worried about is a telephone call. The child sees love, not in the party, but in her father returning her calls. The little things, like returned telephone calls, may not mean much to us, but they mean a lot to those that we love.

A husband may sacrifice his earnings from a second job to buy an expensive gift to please his wife; but perhaps all she really wants is to spend more time in his arms talking. It's the little things. Sometimes it's just the thought that counts. We should all slow down enough to understand, not what we value; rather what our loved ones really value.

Sometimes we can get all of the "big" things right, and strike out because of the little things that promote intimacy and closeness. As we focus on others, God Himself becomes more and more the center of our relationships. As we please others, we learn more about ourselves and more about our need for God.

How Important is God to Human Intimacy?

God is the easiest person of all with whom to be intimate. With God, we cannot falsify the truth. He knows about our tender grapes. God knows more about us than we can ever know about ourselves. He also knows what our next move will be. God even knows what motivates us.

So rather than invite God to get to know us, we have to spend time getting to know Him, above all others. He wants us to invest some time in Him. Our utmost desire should be for a union and oneness with Christ.

Jesus said in John 15:5: *"I am the vine and ye are the branches: He that abideth in me, and I in Him, the same bringeth forth much fruit: for without me ye can do nothing."*

The personal devotion and fervent love shown toward Christ makes the difference in all of our relationships. See Illustration 2-1. Note that as a husband and wife grow closer to God, they simultaneously grow closer to one another.

The one-ness of marriage is exceeded only by the one-ness within the Godhead. It may even be said that all true love grows out of a relationship with God. This truth is fundamental to marriage; no marriage can bring lasting love or "fruit," without it.

Do you remember when you first met the Lord? For those of you who have truly experienced His love, do you remember how you felt when you first found Him, or rather when He first found you?

Remember how you would do anything for Him? Do you remember how you would tell anybody about Him? This is the story of true love.

How Does It Feel to Fall in Love?

To use an earthly example, for those of you who truly love your spouses, do you remember when you first fell in love? Do you remember how you used to feel when you knew that you were going to see your "sweetheart" or your "baby"?

Do you remember how you used to open doors and prepare meals for one another? Do you remember how it felt to tell your friends that you were in love or that you were getting married? I know, for me, it was a beautiful time in my life. I would do anything for my fiancée who later became my wife. Her happiness was my joy!

God is calling on us to remember how it was when we first met Him. Do you remember how God courted you, and how you ran behind God? Do you remember how you used to stay up all night praying and reading His Word? Do you remember how you would tell anybody about Him?

Turn the radio off. Turn the TV off. Turn the cell phone off. Tell your friends and even your "significant other" that you will get back with them. These are the "little foxes" that ruin your budding intimacy with God and, as a result, with others.

> **Try This**
> ....
> ✓ **Make a list of the spiritual practices that you once devoted to God. Why did you stop?**

Go into your "God-place" or your "God-space" and spend some time with Him. As you do this regularly, you will understand the "little things" a lot better. Consequently, when people are attracted to you, you will realize that it's not your physical appearance, it's your relationship with God that is on display.

This means that God is in His proper place in your life, which is first and foremost. Only then we can approach others in the true spirit of intimacy.

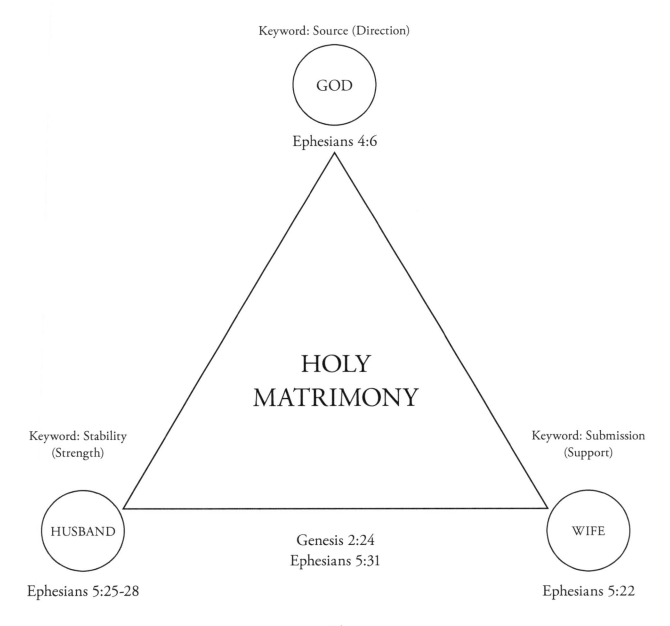

Illustration 2-1
Marriage: A Theological Approach

Keyword: Source (Direction)

GOD

Ephesians 4:6

HOLY
MATRIMONY

Keyword: Stability
(Strength)

Keyword: Submission
(Support)

HUSBAND

WIFE

Genesis 2:24
Ephesians 5:31

Ephesians 5:25-28

Ephesians 5:22

Case Study – Lesson #2

"The Little Things"

"Our vines have tender grapes." Song of Solomon 2:15

Dr. and Mrs. Loving – "A Love Grown Cold"

Lee and Karen Loving seemed to have it all. They were not rich, but they were definitely comfortable. They lived on 40 acres of pristine pineland just outside of Louisville, Kentucky. "God's Country" is what they called it.

When they were younger, their property had been the site of many outdoor revivals and old fashioned tent meetings. There was not a prominent minister, missionary, or itinerant evangelist who had not been invited to their home for fellowship and good, Christian conversation. In a part of the country that was considered "very religious," Lee and Karen were considered the *"religious of the religious."*

Lee, or "Dr. Loving," as he was known to correct the young ministers at the seminary, was recently retired after many years of teaching. Dr. Loving was the foremost authority of New Testament Greek, east of the Mississippi River.

Not that anybody cared about Biblical exegesis anymore; in Dr. Loving's way of thinking, all the young ministers seem to care about is having a large, prominent pulpit, which naturally leads to a large, prominent paycheck.

Even in the halls of academia, there was little love for Biblical truth or orthodoxy. Dr. Loving thought to himself that the state of religious affairs sure did change in a hurry over his 50 years of service – even in the inner sanctums of Baptist life. He constantly thought about his old friends and mentors in seminary and pastoral life who had now gone on to meet the Master.

There were some things that were presently being taught at the seminary that the Presidents of year's past would not have permitted. The seminary's founder, Dr. A. H. Phillips, was quite fond of quoting Romans 1:30, saying that those who strayed from Scripture were *"inventors of evil things."* Now those were men who really loved God! As for Dr. Loving, he had had enough of the "modern way," so he retired without much fanfare.

After all, who among the younger staffers could appreciate a man of his intelligence, technical proficiency and integrity? Dr. Loving's mind was a web of tangled thoughts as he watched movers pack his office. The one bright spot, the one constant encouragement that Dr. Loving, Karen, and his children had over the years, was his beloved, Greater Macedonia.

Yes, he and Karen still had the Greater Macedonia Solid Rock Baptist Church! Over the years, as the level of orthodoxy and right teaching faded at the seminary, Greater Macedonia increased in orthodoxy and held to the sound doctrine of ages past.

While the halls of the seminary were not nearly as filled as they were when Dr. Loving arrived 5 decades ago, in contrast, Greater Macedonia had grown to be the largest Baptist church in the whole State of Kentucky.

People who still desired good, solid Biblical teaching and preaching drove from all over Appalachia and beyond to fill its hallowed halls. So well-known and respected is Greater Macedonia that even Dr. Loving's children, although miles away in Lexington, call it their home church.

Meanwhile, at home, Karen Loving wondered what her life would be like having her husband home every day. She was actually very nervous. "Lovie," as she called him, had changed. Yes, he still loved her no doubt, probably just as much as he did when they met years ago.

Karen knew when she first married him that she would be second to the Church, but the enormity of being "Dr. Loving's wife" was not apparent then. "Lovie" is contacted by preachers, pastors, seminarians, and academicians from all over the world about technical arguments concerning New Testament Greek.

"*It's all Greek to me,*" Karen thought to herself. Still, Karen knew that her husband had changed over the years. He had not always been this way. If no one else knew it, she did. All of the argumentation with other Christians over points of doctrine and then all the "*defending of the faith*" toward unbelievers, had made her "Lovie" somewhat harder, even less feeling.

Her Lovie spent most of his waking hours studying, writing, or counseling other ministerial professionals. He fell asleep in his home office so much that he put a bed in it and slept there quite often.

Karen feared for the thirty or forty younger ministers at Greater Macedonia who looked up to her Lovie – especially Dr. Harper, Lovie's assistant. It wasn't that these ministers were not going to get first class educations from Lovie in such things as Baptist polity and practices, and not to mention a world-class primer in preaching; rather Karen wondered about these ministers' personal lives, in particular, their relationship with the Lord and their wives.

They all seemed to care more about having the correct body of knowledge about God, rather than having a real, actual relationship with God. Dr. Harper carried himself in such a highly polished way – that even for a young man, one would have to wonder whether or not he had ever sinned in any way! Sin seemed so, well, beneath him.

Even when Dr. Harper preached or taught any class, his subject was always about some sin and how it was wrong and people needed to stop doing it. Again, it made you wonder whether or not he had ever done anything less than godly. This very intelligent, articulate, young man seemed so distant, cold even. This was also a part of the change that Karen noticed in Lovie.

Lovie was an expert indeed at thoughts about God, and how to do things properly in the Church. In fact, he would bristle up when someone wouldn't do things the right way, whether it involved the communion table, the pulpit, or any of a number of smaller things in the church.

Karen was beginning to think that Dr. Loving loved, treasured and valued the "rules" and the "thou shalt nots" more than the person who instituted them. Of course, she couldn't argue with the results.

Greater Macedonia had three services and they *all* were full. Generally, the congregants were not in open, habitual sin. They were very moral people who considered themselves saved. Most of them were middle class professionals – like Dr. Loving.

There were dozens of PhDs, medical doctors, engineers, attorneys and CPA's in the church membership and living moral, upstanding lives. They were all so proud to be under the leadership of the Great Dr. Lee Loving and in fellowship with their fellow professionals.

As the legend of Dr. Loving grew, so did the Church. The Church also seemed to grow less close, almost cold, perhaps even formal. The church body knew what was right, they even did what was right.

But Karen wondered if a person could do what is right, and still not be righteous. Karen could even feel it in the way that her husband talked to her. He seemed more distant – less intimate. She sometimes wondered whether he could even "see" her anymore.

Of course, Karen knew that there was no one else; this was something going on inside her Lovie. It had been building slowly over the years, almost imperceptibly at first. Sometimes she wanted to talk to "Lovie," her husband; but she didn't want to risk a lecture from Dr. Loving.

Even his prayers were more formal – at least when he prayed in Karen's presence. When Karen knew some things were bothering him, and that he probably needed to talk, like about his retirement, he would simply quote a Scripture and expect her to dismiss it.

How did these walls go up so quickly, she thought? Leaving him was out of the question, but Karen sure wished that she could reach him. Karen needed to feel the warmth that she once felt toward him. How could a man of his intelligence and Biblical understanding not perceive that the warmth is gone?

Then too…where is Jesus in all of this?

QUESTIONS – LESSON #2

"THE LITTLE THINGS"

"Our vines have tender grapes." Song of Solomon 2:15

1. In your opinion, do the following persons have healthy relationships with God? Please provide evidence for your answers.

   a. Dr. Loving

   _____

   _____

   _____

b. Karen Loving

_____

_____

_____

_____

c. Dr. Harper

_____

_____

_____

_____

2. Is it normal for people to change over time like Dr. Loving has apparently changed? Why or why not?

_____

_____

_____

_____

_____

3. Would you advise Karen to approach her husband? If so, what approach should she take?

_____

_____

_____

_____

4. Can a person's occupation affect their marital relationship? If so, how?

_____

_____

_____

_____

_____

5. Based on Illustration 2-1, is Lee Loving moving closer to God or farther away? What is this doing to his marriage?

_____

_____

_____

_____

_____

6. Over time, how can "little things" help or harm a marriage?

_____

_____

_____

_____

_____

7. What "little things" do you do, to show your spouse that you care?

_____

_____

_____

_____

_____

8. What are some "little things" that are important to you?

    _____

    _____

    _____

    _____

9. Have you shared the "little things" in your answer to the previous question with your spouse?

    _____

    _____

    _____

    _____

10. Why is a good relationship with God foundational to a good relationship with your spouse?

    _____

    _____

    _____

    _____

Lesson #3

"Busy Days and Lonely Nights"

"By night on my bed I sought him whom my soul loveth: I sought him, but I found him not." Song of Solomon 3:1

Loneliness is one of the more dreaded emotions that a person can feel. All of our feelings of low self-esteem and even self-loathing begin with loneliness. Ask anyone who has ever been lonely for an extended period of time, and they will tell you that loneliness hurts.

Let me be clear that loneliness is not defined as the absence of people. A person can be lonely while living in uncomfortably close quarters with others. Loneliness is the feeling of being alone, even when you are not necessarily alone.

The Traumas of Loneliness

To those Christian ladies who are single and lonely, let me be clear in telling you that marriage is not the answer, or the "cure-all," for loneliness. There are literally millions of Christian wives who are married and also miserable. They live day after day in homes where they wish their husbands would simply talk to them. They share meals. They share the television. They share the bed. They even share the kids. Still, they are lonely.

Loneliness may also be defined as "not being understood." Quite often the emotional traumas of childhood and the long shadows of dysfunctional families follow us into adulthood. See Illustrations 5-1 and 5-2.

How many ladies have been molested and have never discussed it with anyone? How many sexual assaults took place in the family home and were never discussed,

> **Try This**
> ·······································
> ✓ **Ask your spouse to tell you something about themselves that you don't already know.**

let alone reported? How many ladies have been damaged emotionally by early abortions? Then, too, there are the feelings of abandonment and isolation experienced early in life when one or both of the parents are not present in the home.

All of these childhood traumas follow us through life and lead to our having "secrets," which cause our behavior to be misunderstood. To be consistently misunderstood leads to loneliness.

How many wives have longed to tell their husbands the secrets of their childhood homes? How many ladies who are approaching middle age have "sudden memories" of what life was like as a child or some negative, life-denying event that has heretofore been buried in the decades past? Why do many of our relationships fall into the same negative pattern?

Not Being Appreciated

The long tentacles of loneliness are not limited to being misunderstood. A person may be understood, and yet, his or her sacrifice or efforts go unappreciated. Since the value of such a noble virtue as self-sacrifice is subjective, it may indeed go unappreciated and lead to loneliness.

After all, a person can be at the pinnacle of earthly achievement – the corner office, the right title, the right car, the right neighborhood – and, yet, be all alone. No one really understands what it took to get there, or what it takes to stay there.

Sometimes, it is hard to put into words what husbands and wives sacrifice to maintain their present standard of living. Loneliness may be birthed through not being appreciated – especially for the effort that a person puts forth – whether they are married or not.

In Whose Presence Do You Undress?

Marital intimacy, in my own words, is when we fully undress spiritually and emotionally in the presence of our spouses. This is the 21st century meaning of Genesis 2:25. This verse reads, *"And they were both naked, the man and his wife, and were not ashamed."*

Most men and women of this day have been physically naked in the presence of far too many people in their lives, but have yet to get undressed spiritually and emotionally in the presence of spouses. Do not let this fact shock you. Think about it for a moment.

Sometimes we will be more at ease with total strangers, or people we just met than with our spouses. After all, this is the age of casual sex and "easy" intimacy.

> **Try This**
> ....
> ✓ **Set aside a time to just "dream" with your spouse.**
> ✓ **Leave all negativity behind.**

Sometimes, it is easier to share your "tender-grapes" with someone you just met, because they still hold the promise of being "perfect" or your "ideal." In contrast, you know the many flaws of your mate, and these flaws serve as barriers to intimacy.

Relational intimacy is not easy. Single men and women, this should only be done within the bond of marriage. You don't expose your heart to someone you just met – even if it does "feel right." Don't tell your dreams to people who are just "passing through" your life. Tell your dreams to those who plan to put down roots with you.

It's easier to talk to someone you just met, especially when you have had a few drinks, or when you are feeling really lonely. Yet, you have to resist this tendency, especially if you are holding on for something real and meaningful.

Let's Talk About It

Again, for those who are in committed relationships, it is not easy to be intimate emotionally. In fact, for most, the physical act of sex is easier than undressing emotionally. After all, most of us have been through so many things in our lives – many of them negative – that we are embarrassed to even *think* about some of them.

If we have tried to put these experiences out of our minds and bury them deep in the dark past, and yet they still trouble us, that is a good sign that we really need to talk about them.

> **Try This**
> ....
> ✓ **Set aside a time each day to both talk and listen to your spouse.**

We are fearful of talking about these things, because how many of us truly know how to express such complex and powerful thoughts? If we were led to express our experiences to others, we really wouldn't know how to begin. So expressing these thoughts verbally is definitely an obstacle.

Can I Handle Real Talk?

Marital intimacy requires a certain level of maturity in both the husband and the wife. How does a woman tell her husband that some of her self-acceptance issues are due to traumas that occurred in her early childhood (e.g., incest, molestation, rape)?

Some men are not mature enough for that level of intimacy. Some women want to talk, but I can imagine a man saying, *"I didn't want to know that."* Worse yet, some men would not say anything in response to what their wives shared. The answer of most men would be even more silence.

Most of us who desire to be in relationships don't know how to deal with real human beings who have real emotions and who want to express them fully.

Look at it this way, most of us fell in love with a fiction or a person who is not real. We barely knew who we were when we got married, let alone who we were marrying.

How many of us have looked back and secretly thought: *"I wasn't in love when I got married"* or *"I didn't know what the heck I was doing!"*

Yet all life grows toward wholeness. Women want to heal. They really want to talk about the abortion, the incest, the infidelity, the hurt caused by a parent, or even the hurt caused by an old boyfriend, or an ex-husband. Our fictional wife, Jane, whose story is discussed in the Case Study to Lesson #5, would, over time, want to discuss the issues within the circles of Illustration 5-1.

To Share Her Secret, Is to Share Her Life

Men, this is why women talk to other women, sometimes, instead of talking to us. This is why they have such strong ties to sisters, aunts, cousins, and friends. These people already know their secrets. The women confide in them because they don't know whether we can handle some of what they will lay on us.

And women, yes, you are right. You have to be careful in studying your husband to know what you can tell him and when. He may not be ready to hear the whole story, regardless of what his mouth says. He has to grow into that maturity.

A man will stop talking to you intimately because you told him something that happened ten years ago that he finds hard to deal with – even though he didn't even know you. Men, a part of our assignment in marriage is to ultimately become the repository for our wives' secrets.

Husbands, Are You Trustworthy?

The people that our wives really love and trust are the ones to whom they tell their secrets. In Jane's case (see Illustration 5-1), she has much to share. To whom does your wife tell her secrets? If your wife had something really important to say that would undress her emotionally, to whom would she go?

Are you the type of man who can talk to your wife about matters that don't revolve around you? Can you stay awake long enough and show enough interest in her thoughts, her fears, her dreams and her desires? These are the "little things" that mean so much.

Can you keep your hands off of her long enough to truly listen *to* her? Sex, the elephant who is always in the room, doesn't cure loneliness. Affection and physical closeness do not cure the complex issues of abandonment and self-hatred.

> **Husbands, Try This**
>
> ✓ **Make a mental list of the times that you have proven yourself to be trustworthy with the concerns of another.**

Ephesians 5:25-29 reads: *"And you husbands must love your wives with the same love Christ showed the church. He gave up His life for her to make her holy and clean, washed by baptism and God's word. He did this to present her to Himself as a glorious church without spot or wrinkle or any other blemish."*

"Instead she will be holy and without fault. In the same way, husbands ought to love their wives as they love their own bodies. For a man loves himself when he loves his wife; no one hates his own body but lovingly cares for it, just as Christ cares for His body, which is the church."

Now that is a tall assignment for a man. Oftentimes, men focus on what their wives should be doing – "obeying" and "following" – but the husband has the tougher chore – "loving as Christ loved."

For instance, if a wife is not becoming more and more "one" with her husband in Christ, see Illustration 2-1, then she is hardening spiritually and emotionally against him.

This hardening does not occur intentionally, it is an unconscious process. Women and wives can be hardened by the day-to-day subtle neglect that they experience at the hands of their husbands.

> **Husbands, Try This**
> ✓ **Truly accept something about your spouse that you don't like, in the spirit of "loving as Christ loved."**

Whereas wives were once joyous to see you when you got home, and it was a joy to cook for you, and a joy to share your bed, now it has slowly become a chore.

It is a chore because wives are no longer the tender ladies that you met and married. When you are lonely in a marriage, you cry a lot because you are tender. Men, eventually, your wife's tears will dry. The tender grapes, if not reciprocated, will slowly give way to an inner hardening process.

Honey, Please Don't Make Me Harden

Have you ever seen a lady whose outward appearance was so hard that you knew somebody, somewhere, had done something really bad to her? Women and wives become hardened emotionally due to the lack of intimacy in what should be, and could be, the most intimate of relationships. Their hardness is the only emotional protection that they have to keep them from getting hurt even more.

When the tears dried, women secretly vowed that they would not let you, or any other man, hurt them anymore. So she is not surprised that you no longer bring her flowers, or treat her special.

She is no longer surprised that you don't say, "I love you" anymore. She learns to live in her hardened shell; dying a lonely, slow, emotional, death because her "husband" would not give her the true companionship that she needed to live.

Ephesians 5:31 reads in the KJV, "*For this cause shall a man leave his father and mother, and shall be joined unto his wife and they two shall be one flesh.*"

To Know Him, Is to Love Him

Women, there are some things required of you as well. God instills in men the desire to be one flesh. Now, sometimes, men take this rather literally in their desire to be together only physically. This is one of his greatest attractions to you.

But as men grow in their understanding of themselves and their understanding of the Lord, they too have hurts they want to talk about, but sometimes wives are too judgmental to listen.

Some can't listen because they are too busy expressing their opinions before he can even get everything out. If it is hard for women to express issues that isolate them and make them feel lonely, then it is especially hard for men. Talking about "feelings" is unchartered territory for most men.

Can you imagine our fictional husband, John (see Illustration 5-2), expressing some of the hurt in his circles? So men generally tread lightly in this area, looking for the first hint of criticism.

No man wants to talk to his partner if he believes that his partner is only listening to criticize him. If you are never on his side, he will not like talking to you.

Men, like women, are already self-conscious about their feelings. Men, too, have hurts from the past, again see Illustration 5-2. Most of these hurts involve women — whether it is his mother or an old flame.

Women, if you want intimacy and a true spiritual connection with your husband, sometimes you have to listen to him talk about his old girl-friend, his ex-wife, or even his child by another woman.

You can't call a woman whom you've never met out of her name, and then tell your husband, "*I don't want to hear that!*" If your husband needs to talk about it, to whom would you suggest he talk?

And wife, how can you be angry with a child who had nothing to do with how he or she was conceived? This type of unbridled anger *kills* marital intimacy. After all, our fictional husband, John, did father a son in high school (see Illustration 5-2). Must he pay for it forever?

Your husband doesn't talk to you because you are easily upset. When a man opens up, he does it a little at a time to see if it's safe to continue to open up.

You say that you are lonely because your husband doesn't talk, but sometimes your husband doesn't open up to you because you have not reached the level of maturity where you can talk about things *without* blowing up.

Your husband may sit stewing over a beer or watching a ballgame. You may believe that his mind is going no further than the beer or the ballgame, but you are wrong! Men think deep thoughts about their relationships – past, present, and yes, even future ones. The question is, can he talk to you?

Avoid the Big Fight

The other reason that men do not undress emotionally before their wives is because some women will use the discussion as ammunition in a later fight. They will quietly gather information, knowing full well that they will use it later.

Some things in a marriage are off-limits, even, and especially when you are fighting. When a husband shares his secrets, these secrets are not to be made fun of or repeated. If you want to hurt your husband and destroy his manhood, you can do it by repeating his secrets.

> **Wives, Try This**
>
> ✓ **Become the bigger person by immediately humbling yourself in times of heated disagreement.**

If you make fun of him, or bring it back up when you are angry, or repeat it to someone else, you will destroy the tender grapes in your marriage. Your husband is trying to become one with you on a different level – other than physically.

Women, have you grown enough emotionally to listen to your husband talk about whatever he wants to talk about and be non-judgmental? Or are you the type of person that your husband needs an attorney when he is around you, because you will use whatever he says as evidence later when you disagree?

Additionally, are you the type of woman who wants your husband to open up to you, but you will not open up to him? Have you been hurt so much in marriage that you have given up on marital intimacy and true spiritual union? Aren't you ready to finally experience the sacredness of married sex?

Even though marriage is described in Scripture as a "one-flesh" arrangement (see Illustration 7-1), in reality, our marriages have, at times, seemed more like armed camps.

Talking the Talk

How else can we describe an arrangement whereby men and women who once pledged to love one another can go for days without even speaking to one another? Yes, single people, this is what marriage is like when God is no longer the center, and the little things are being neglected.

A "grunt" now passes for "*good morning.*" Mumbling or even a slammed door passes for, "*I'm going to work now.*" Over time, so many hurtful things have occurred in our marriages, that we have forgotten about marital intimacy, which begins with communication.

True communication has to be restored in most marriages. "*Pass me the milk*" or "*what's for dinner?*" does not count as true communication. A playful tap on the backside in the hallway, also does not pass for true marital intimacy. Men are lonely, and women are lonely, too. God brought us together for true intimacy and tenderness.

When we stopped communicating, we damaged the "tender grapes" in our marriages. Every moment of every day that you are at odds *slowly* kills your intimacy.

Think about all those days over the course of your marriage when you were not talking at all. Each day you were not speaking to one another represents a day in which you both were learning to live lonely.

I call it self-training in the art of marital warfare. You thought you were doing things to hurt your spouse, and you were. But since the Bible teaches that you are one-flesh in marriage (see Illustration 7-1), each day you reached out to hurt your spouse, you were also hurting yourself.

Each day that you were not speaking, you were making your spouse "harder" and making yourself "harder" also. You thought you were going to hurt your spouse and bring him or her into submission,

> **Try This**
>
> ✓ **Name one thing that you have done to contribute to a "less than Godly" environment in your home.**

when in actuality, since you are one-flesh, you were hurting both of you, and your children, as well as destroying the tenderness of marriage.

Note that all parties in a home are spiritually interdependent, such that what happens to one, ultimately happens to them all. Study the three points of the triangle in Illustration 7-1.

Though everything may seem fine now, trust me, the scar tissue from those episodes is still present. We may have come out of our shells some, but the hardened shell of loneliness is still there from all those days of barely speaking.

Since the shell of loneliness is still there, we are hardened in some places. Even though we may peek our heads out from time to time, we can go back into the shell at any time. Most married people know that you can bring up a certain conversation, and it may cause you both to stop speaking for a season.

Walking the Walk

To get back the intimacy in your marriage will require spiritual rehab. As most of you know, rehab is slow and painful. Most of us expect to say, *"I'm sorry,"* get on our knees, and pray for forgiveness, and everything will be fine. That is true –if you didn't spend all those days barely speaking and learning to be married and lonely.

First, all of the past has to be cleaned up. That will take some time. Every day you spend barely speaking or even being deceitful, is a day that you must spend learning to talk and being tender all over again.

You didn't become married and lonely overnight, and you will not get your marriage back together overnight. No big trip, no new car, no surprise dinner or romantic getaway will bring back tenderness and marital intimacy. Focus on the small acts of love and compassion that say, *"I care."*

"I love you," will come. For now, concentrate on compassion – *I care.* Instead of focusing on the romance, focus on being a friend. Rather than talking, focus on listening. Learn to take a new and true interest in your spouse.

It is the little things that destroy intimacy and create marital loneliness, and it's the little things that will reignite the fires of relationship. God has placed within men and women the ability to experience *true* spiritual union, and what it really means to be "one flesh." This is what makes anything less, so *un*satisfying.

Anything less than God says we can be, will lead to an experience of loneliness and the feeling of "what could have been."

> **Try These Tips**
>
> ✓ **Keep a journal and record your daily thoughts.**
>
> ✓ **Forgive your spouse for the last thing he/she did to hurt you.**
>
> ✓ **Ask your spouse when was the last time you hurt his/her feelings.**

CASE STUDY – LESSON #3

"BUSY DAYS AND LONELY NIGHTS"

"By night on my bed I sought him whom my soul loveth: I sought him, but I found him not." Song of Solomon 3:1

Sophie Clark – "Sophie's Soul Searching"

Sophie was always thinking about something it seems. She had often been told by friends and lovers alike that she was too *"into her head"* or *"too analytical."* Even when her body was resting, her mind was still busy. Sophie had all kinds of mental checklists. It seems as if she was responsible for so much. *"Is retirement supposed to be this busy?"* she thought.

Sophie was not introverted, mind you; she was usually the center of attention, but in a quiet sort of way. She just thought too much about things when she was alone. Not that

Sophie minded being alone. She was practically raised as an only child. Her older sister and sole sibling, Cynthia, was 15 years older. Cynthia was "grown and gone" by the time Sophie entered grade school.

Of course, Sophie was naturally smart and quick witted – some would even say that she was gifted. By the time she finished her formal schooling, she had two degrees and had finished both with honors.

Sophie was proud of her achievements and always prided herself on her academic ability, quick wit, and keen mind. Sophie was also quite beautiful in a very penetrating sort of way. Hers was a dark beauty – with dark, nearly flawless skin; dark, almost mysterious eyes; and, to top it off, she had long, dark, curly hair to match her long, dark, lovely legs.

Perhaps her life would have been different if she and her sister Cynthia had been closer in age; then maybe Sophie would have had more adult supervision and guidance when she was younger. Sophie's natural, dark beauty made her the object of older men's affections, even from an early age.

Native intelligence and blinding beauty allowed Sophie to feed her youthful lusts. She discovered early on that raw sex appeal has power. It seemed as though Sophie could get exactly what she wanted from most men – even though she was raped once by a married man.

Sophie never told her mother. In fact, she never told anyone. Mostly, it was her pride. She couldn't stand to think that someone actually outsmarted her and got what they wanted without her getting what she wanted!

Sophie's mother, Myra Clark, was previously married to Eugene Clark, Cynthia's father. Although Sophie's last name is also Clark, she has some doubt as to whether Eugene Clark is her real father.

Eugene and Myra went through a stormy, nasty divorce when Sophie was still in diapers. Eugene Clark was a very fair skinned man with straight hair who passed away many years ago. Although Cynthia got a chance to know him, Sophie didn't.

Sophie always surmised that if Eugene Clark were her father (and that's a big "if") then she had to be the "accident," because she was born so late in her mother's life. Some in the community used to whisper that Sophie was not Eugene's child at all; rather Myra Clark was so promiscuous, even when she was in her forties, that Sophie could belong to one of a number of men.

Whoever her father is, he must have been really attractive because Sophie's looks easily eclipsed those of both her older sister and her mother. Then, too, there had also been rumors that the Clark's divorced precisely because of Sophie. One look at the child, and everyone knew that somebody had some explaining to do.

Sophie was never told this, but as a child she could almost sense it. She always felt like an outsider. There always seemed to be something a "little different" about her. Her mother talked about Cynthia as if Cynthia were royalty. In fact, Sophie could remember her mother saying that the years that she spent with Cynthia and Eugene were the best of her life.

Sophie was smart and certainly good looking, but she always got treated like she wasn't wanted by her older mother, almost an interruption in her otherwise idyllic home life. Sophie never really had any experience with a father figure of any type – only her mother's broken dreams.

Looking back, Sophie realized that she managed to channel all the rejection and loneliness that she felt as a child into her studies, and then to her professional life. This paid off in a long, established career as a government engineer in Galveston.

Over a period of thirty years, Sophie served the Government well and was promoted regularly. She became known as a more than capable professional who was one of the best project engineers that the Galveston office had ever seen.

Of course, over the years Sophie had her dalliances, even on the job. In fact, she ended up marrying a Government employee from another city – Alberto Vinny. They met at an engineering conference in Salt Lake City.

Alberto was every bit as intelligent as Sophie, and unfortunately, every bit as sexually immoral as well. They both hid their indiscretions beneath a veneer of intelligence and feigned professionalism. They were living the life!

In the circles in which they traveled, there was a way to do everything. Although Alberto was not especially handsome, he was super-smart, well-respected, and had just enough "street-daring" to make him quite attractive sexually to Sophie. There was something about him that seemed so familiar.

As for Alberto's perspective, he just had to have Sophie. He told her that a beauty like hers was rare. Alberto read long portions of Shakespeare to Sophie. They wined, dined, and courted on the Government's account. He even sang to her – in Italian – which he spoke fluently.

He was not content just to romance her, he wanted to marry her and have children. For the first time in her life, Sophie actually wanted a man all her own. She wanted to be loved and taken care of. She was also ecstatic that this man wanted her – not as a mistress or a plaything, but as his wife.

Sophie thought to herself years later, "*Why is it that I can know exactly what a woman is thinking before she opens her mouth, but I was just plain stupid when it came down to Alberto!*" She certainly was fooled by Alberto, and who knows, maybe Alberto even fooled himself into thinking that he loved Sophie and would forsake all other women.

They were not married two years before they divorced because of his infidelity. No children were conceived in the marriage. It is said that in war, "truth" is the first casualty, but in Alberto and Sophie's short marriage, "trust" was the first casualty.

Even though they were legally married, Sophie felt like she was raped – again. She was hurt that she allowed Alberto to get so close to her, closer than any man had ever gotten. Then too, she was just plain stupefied when she learned that Alberto's mistress was little more than a file clerk in the Salt Lake City office.

All of that was years ago – but still fresh in Sophie's mind. Ever the dark, smart, beauty; she was lonesome. Outwardly, she was well off, but inwardly, she was tormented by memories.

Her mother had recently passed away. They never reconciled. Sophie still wasn't sure of who her father is. Cynthia was living in a nursing home in another city, slowly losing her mind to dementia.

Of course, Sophie still had the occasional tryst, but it always ended the same way. Sophie could not trust men. Whether they were older men who were on her level socially, or even younger, ambitious men who saw her as a trophy, she just couldn't open her heart to them.

Her intelligence and beauty were barriers that kept most people from getting close to her. As long as she worked and kept things in order, even in church, she could keep people from really knowing the real her. *"If they only knew, she thought…"* Sophie was desperately lonely.

Sophie always attended church. It was somewhat expected in the South. In retirement, she went more out of habit and to be needed. She was the Chair-woman of the Church Trustee Board, which was unheard of.

Sophie, ever the mental problem solver, thought that religion was for the young and idealistic and those who were really old, in poor health, and who needed comforting thoughts.

Although she prayed from time to time, she never really accepted the reality of the Christian God. Sure, she knew that there was a higher power, but she wasn't much for Christian doctrine – being born again, repenting, and confessing sins –although she would never say it openly.

She just quietly enjoyed the services and the fellowship. Her church was more formal than most, which was to her liking, since she wanted to choose whom to invite in her life and at what time. But lately, Sophie has been disturbed, perhaps even distressed. She has been plagued by self-doubt.

The normally sure, radiant, confident Sophie is now doing some soul searching. She felt empty. She had nothing in this world – no family connection, no spouse, and no children. What she wanted most was companionship and given her good looks and intelligence, she wondered aloud: *"What's wrong with me? Why isn't anyone attracted to me?"* She had the name, she also had the experience, she was in the right circles socially, but she still felt empty.

Sophie would never mention her feelings of inadequacy to anyone. She had never had any good experiences opening up to anyone. So she refused to talk to anyone – not her friends, not her pastor, or anyone else.

"Some things you just don't mention," Sophie thought to herself. Sophie was content to go on and figure this "life" thing out. She was strong, and she would make it!

Questions – Lesson #3

"Busy Days and Lonely Nights"

"By night on my bed I sought him whom my soul loveth: I sought him, but I found him not." Song of Solomon 3:1

1. Does Sophie have a solid relationship with God? Why or why not?

    _____

    _____

    _____

    _____

    _____

2. Imagine Sophie's life sketched in the form of Illustration 5-1. Now answer the following questions.

   a. How has Sophie's background helped to contribute to the person that she is?

   _____

   _____

   _____

   _____

   b. What part has loneliness played?

   _____

   _____

   _____

   _____

3. Why do you think Sophie is doing some soul-searching at this point in her life? What may be some of the results of her soul-searching?

   _____

   _____

   _____

   _____

   _____

4. With regard to her loneliness, what would you advise Sophie?

   _____

   _____

   _____

   _____

   _____

5. In your opinion, could Sophie and Alberto's marriage have been saved? Why or why not?

_____

_____

_____

_____

_____

6. How well do you listen to others?

_____

_____

_____

_____

_____

7. Ask someone with whom you are close, whether or not you listen well. Do they agree with your assessment in Question 6 above?

_____

_____

_____

_____

_____

8. Based on the information in Lesson #3, name some types of loneliness.

_____

_____

_____

_____

_____

9. For those who are single, how does loneliness during certain seasons accomplish God's purposes?

_____

_____

_____

_____

_____

10. For those who are married, what are some of the ways that Lesson #3 suggests to restore marital intimacy?

_____

_____

_____

_____

_____

Lesson #4

"The History of Your Heart"

"Keep thy heart with all diligence; for out of it are the issues of life." Proverbs 4:23

In the midst of our relationships, we have all wondered: *"How did we get here?"* "Here" is usually a place of extreme emotional crisis and testing.

Most people are content to examine and, if necessary, re-examine all of the happenings and events of the present relationship. What is really needed is an examination of all of our past relationships leading up to the present one.

Yes, we have all wondered, "How did we get here?" Well, the best way to tell a story is from the beginning. The story of our emotional lives begins with the seat of emotion: the heart.

My Physical Heart

I am not a cardiologist, but from a physical perspective, I am told that every human heart has an anatomical and biological history. Medically, the stresses and strains of life leave a demonstrable, physical affect on the human heart. Scar tissue, the constriction of blood vessels, and leaky valves are all on display in the heart.

Now, from a less biologically technical perspective, years of bad dietary habits (fried chicken, fried fish, fried pork, fried cheese, re-fried beans, salty ham, ham hocks, and pork skins), all show up in the fatty tissue in and around the heart. Oftentimes, it is the heart and its attendant circulatory system, that gives a person trouble later in life.

So efficient is the heart in capturing what goes on in the body, that a cardiologist can examine a heart and determine what kind of diet the person has, the approximate age of that person, what type of life that person has lived (whether a more stressful or a less stressful life) and whether or not he or she has had any type of significant coronary event, such as a heart attack. Each physical heart tells a great deal of the history of that person.

My Spiritual Heart

From a spiritual perspective, "heart-breaks," "hurt-hearts," "heavy-hearts," "hard hearts," and "sad hearts," are all phrases that indicate the affects that life has had on the spiritual heart.

Just as your physical heart has a history, so does your "spiritual" heart. If you have ever been hurt by anybody, anywhere, at any-time, the emotional trauma associated with that hurt is recorded in your spiritual heart.

My Hurting Heart

Every woman who has ever trusted a man with her heart (whether her daddy, her boyfriend, or even her husband) who then later hurt her, has that hurt recorded in her heart. See Illustration 5-1 for an example of personal hurts that a woman may have in her heart.

She may be sixty now, married with several grown children, and even some grand-children, but if she was hurt when she was sixteen, that hurt is still present, if it has not been dealt with properly.

Men who have been hurt by their mothers due to abandonment or neglect, or hurt emotionally by another woman (such as a wife or girlfriend), also have hurt in their hearts. See Illustration 5-2, for an example of personal hurts that a man may have in his heart.

> **Try This**
>
> ✓ **Have a "heart to heart" with an older person. Inquire about some of the hurtful things that occurred earlier in their lives. Ask them how they coped.**
>
> ✓ **Leave all negativity behind.**

A man may not ever discuss the hurt. He may even believe himself to be "over it," or that it doesn't matter. Yet, this hurt is still recorded in his heart. It affects everything he does as it relates to the opposite sex.

The "you" that you know of as "you" (with all of your idiosyncrasies and self-delusions), finds its center in your heart. All that you have been, where you have been, and what you have been through, your fears as well as happenings or events that you dread, are contained in your heart.

Even when you forget, your heart remembers. You know it remembers the past when it sends you very strong emotions and feelings about what is happening in the present.

The Heart Remembers

For example, sometimes you can meet a person, and you instantly don't like him or her. You have not met this person before. He or she has not done anything to you for you to dislike them, but you do. You knew that you disliked this person from the moment you laid eyes on them.

There is an emotional reaction to this person that does not make logical sense. That is your heart remembering another person who may look like this person, sound like them, act like them, or be in a position of authority like them.

The heart remembers a person who hurt you, who was just like this person. That is your heart saying, *"Beware of this person."* The heart sends you that message because the heart retains the pain from what happened the last time – even when you don't consciously remember.

When you meet a person and say to yourself, *"I know his type,"* or *"I know her type,"* that is your heart pulling from its history of hurts. There is something in your heart that causes you to say that.

The heart is the seat of human personality. This is what the writer seems to indicate in Proverbs 4:23. *"Keep thy heart with all diligence; for out of it are the issues of life."* We all see and experience the world through our hearts. The heart is also the tape recorder and preserver of all that makes up a person, emotionally.

You Are What Your Heart Says You Are

You are who you are because of what is in your heart. You feel the way you do because of what is in your heart. Do not neglect the strength of what happens in the innermost parts of a person. This is why the writer warns the reader to *"keep"* or *"guard"* the heart.

Whatever negative, destructive emotion gets lodged in your heart, is hard to get out. Only God can remove it. The strongest sins in Scripture are those emotional sins that get lodged or stuck in the heart.

Some of these emotional sins include hatred, bitterness, envy, jealousy, anger, malice, un-forgiveness, and pride. These are emotional sins rather than particular acts of sin.

In other words, something can happen to you that has a strong emotional component to it (e.g., rape, incest, abortion, abandonment, and extreme favoritism), and that emotional component is what gets stored in your heart.

Stored Hurt Is Sin

Stored hurt becomes sin in your heart. That hurt is also what hardens your heart. The stored hurt affects your thinking (i.e., you are more likely to believe things that are not true because it resonates within your sinful heart).

Hurt also affects how you treat others. You are more likely to keep people at a distance, because you think everybody wants to hurt you. The stored hurt in your heart affects how you look outwardly at your world. You are more likely to perceive everyday events negatively. Your stored hurt also affects how people treat you, as they are more likely to view you as being "hard-hearted."

When people exhibit behavior toward you that is baffling, they too are being driven by a past hurt that they allowed in their hearts. God judges the condition of the heart.

Release Your Hurt

The only release for this "sin and hurt" is confession and forgiveness. Because the hurt is in our hearts, we are less likely to ask God for forgiveness, or to even recognize that there is a problem. Yet, when we look outwardly at life, the hurt that is in our hearts colors all that we see and feel.

For instance, a woman may not be able to really open up to her husband at the deepest levels of her heart, because there are some hurts that are still there.

Because she has been hurt by someone else, she involuntarily cuts her husband off emotionally. She has not properly dealt with that hurt. Sometimes, a wife can't love her husband at the level that she really wants to love him. She can only go so far.

Now she and her husband may get along fine for years. Her husband may even think that it's him, but it's not him. It's her. She has not yet dealt with the hurt. She hasn't had to deal with it. She has been blaming her husband because she sees life and her relationship with her current husband, through the lens of the hurt that happened in another relationship years ago. When there is difficulty in a relationship, oftentimes, the way forward is to go back.

> **Try These Tips**
>
> ✓ **Confess to your spouse something that happened to you long ago.**
>
> ✓ **Ask your spouse to say a special prayer for you.**
>
> ✓ **Name one quality about yourself that you don't like that makes you hard to get along with.**

In addition to containing the issues of the past, your heart also contains the seeds or potentialities of the future. Your heart contains all that you can be. It contains where you really want to go in life, and where you will actually go in life; your hopes, dreams, ambitions, and all of your potential.

Each of these aspects (past events – *"the things I have been through,"* as well as future life potentials – *"what I have my heart set on"*) is contained right now in our hearts.

Held Back Because of Hurts

The writer asks us to *"guard"* or *"keep"* our hearts because *"out of it are the issues of life."* The themes of my whole life are contained right now in my heart.

Have you ever had the feeling that "something" or "somebody" was holding you back? Have you ever had a dream that you wanted to achieve and, yet, you always seemed to fall short?

Why is it that you always have "issues" when dealing with other people? Why are you so emotional and steadfast about some things? Why are there some things that you will not let go?

These are all issues of the heart. Sometimes these issues don't paint a pretty picture. Since God Himself should be at the center of our lives (see Illustration 2-1), we are called upon to constantly confess our hurts and forgive those who hurt us. If not, we will continually view and evaluate others based on our emotional baggage from the past.

> **Try This**
>
> ✓ **Pray daily for God to search and research your heart for hidden hurts.**

As we release the past, oftentimes, we will have startling revelations about the present. One of the more common revelations is that we chose the person we are with for all the wrong reasons. Perhaps they provided something that we needed at the time. Maybe they provided emotional security during a time that we felt especially vulnerable. Of course, some of us realize that we married spouses similar to our opposite-sex parent.

Dealing with the contents of our hearts can be scary. It is a confrontation with the truth about our situation. Sadly, this is precisely why so many men and women do not dare to delve into their hearts. They have "too much to lose," they reason to themselves.

Growing Past Your Own Limitations

Some have even placed all of their hope and trust in the current spouse, to the neglect of the long-standing emotional issues of the heart. Yet, if the journey into the heart is not undertaken, a person will not grow past his or her own limitations, and neither will their relationship.

This is how adulterous relationships get started: a man courts one woman for romance, but is married to another for security. The relationship with the wife will only grow so far; she will never know that portion of her husband that he shares with his mistress.

Try This

✓ **Make a list of those to whom you have exposed your whole heart. Are you satisfied with the list?**

Likewise, the mistress will not know that portion of "her man," who is married to another. Both the wife and the mistress think they know the man, but they don't. For his part, the man doesn't have to expose the totality of his heart to either the wife or the mistress.

The true issue is not what his wife lacks; nor what his mistress provides; it's his heart. This man will always have something vital lacking in his relationships because he refuses to confront the truth of the history of his heart.

The result is that he cannot become "one-flesh" with his wife because he has 'secrets' from the past that he cannot share with her, or even face himself. The 'secrets' are the source of his pain and hurt.

Because God placed it within all of us to desire this "one-flesh" union, our imaginary man tries to find solace and companionship in the arms of a mistress, but the deception involved in this relationship will also limit what he can share.

Thus, the man is limited in all of his relationships, especially the relationship with that person who should be at the center of his heart: God.

CASE STUDY – LESSON #4

"THE HISTORY OF YOUR HEART"

"Keep thy heart with all diligence; for out of it are the issues of life." Proverbs 4:23

Ruthie Collins – "Ruthie's Dilemma"

Ruthie Collins is a new convert. She joined the 2ⁿᵈ Pentecostal True Believers Apostolic Church in Bear Creek, Georgia, nearly four years ago. She was invited there by one of her high school classmates – Irma Jane Smith. *Irma Jane was always a "little strange" back in those days*, Ruthie thought to herself.

2nd Pentecostal was considered one of those "sanctified" churches, and it sure showed in Irma Jane. They used to call her "Plain Jane" in school because of the paucity of makeup and other beauty enhancements that she wore – or rather didn't wear. She wore mostly long skirts and dresses as well.

While most teen-agers were enjoying all the social aspects of high school (social drinking, social flirting, and just plain being social), Irma Jane spent most of her time with other members of 2nd Pentecostal on church retreats, or as Ruthie imagined, somewhere either "praying and studying, or studying and praying."

Of course, Irma Jane was quite a personality; you just had to get to know her. She was friendly and of more than average intelligence. She knew her Bible, too. Ruthie found that although Irma Jane was teased for being a member of the "sanctified" church, Irma Jane could tease mercilessly as well.

When they were in high school, she always teased Ruthie about being a member of a church where they didn't believe their own book – the Bible – and where the preacher didn't even believe his own sermons. When Ruthie protested that this wasn't true, Irma Jane would ask, *"Well, why doesn't anybody in the Greater Solid Rock B-A-P-T-I-S-T church obey? Sounds like the Greater Solid 'Crumbling' Rock to me!"*

All Ruthie could do was laugh. She was no match for Irma Jane in Biblical or moral discussions, and they both knew it. How did she get so smart! In fact, Irma Jane was Ruthie's confidant.

Of course, Irma Jane didn't attend the dances at school or any of the after-hours parties. Her parents hardly let her attend anything where there was limited supervision. So Irma Jane wasn't Ruthie's "public friend," although they were friendly in public.

The years passed. Irma Jane helped Ruthie in the aftermath of an abortion. Although Irma Jane protested the abortion, Ruthie's boyfriend, Rick, had the last say. Rick was Ruthie's first serious love.

Although Rick and Ruthie were still in college, they spent so much time together it was like they were married. To Ruthie, Rick put the sun, the moon and all the stars to shame. So when Rick insisted that the baby be aborted – it was.

Just a few weeks later, it was Ruthie and Rick back out on the town again. The "good times" for Ruthie and Rick continued until just shortly before graduation. Rick dropped the news: He had accepted a job in Bessemer, South Carolina, and he was leaving – without Ruthie. It was Irma Jane who prayed Ruthie through this tough time.

It was also Irma Jane who invited Ruthie to church. She didn't tell Ruthie that she wasn't a committed believer, she didn't have to. Ruthie was originally baptized at an early age by Pastor Brown in the Greater Solid Rock Baptist Church.

Although she was faithful in church attendance and ministry participation, she was never as committed as Irma Jane. Then too, nobody in Greater Solid Rock was very committed to anything: although they had "good service" and overflow crowds.

The Greater Solid Rock Baptist Church counted most of the Black middle class in its membership. While 2nd Pentecostal and its half empty pews were basically ignored; Greater Solid Rock was always the hub of community activity.

Large funerals, large weddings, large crowds, they were the "G-R-E-A-T-E-R" Solid Rock. Irma Jane would always press Ruthie to confide in members of her own church, especially her pastor. Ruthie just wouldn't do it. She had too much respect for Pastor Brown.

In fact, she grew up having a crush on him. Everyone was in awe of him. She could tell that some of the women, young and old, also had secret crushes on him. And who wouldn't? He was tall, handsome, and could sing like a song bird!

Although there were always rumors about his fidelity to his wife, that didn't matter to most women. Sister Brown wasn't too much to look at, although she was very sweet. The women thought the Pastor could do better, especially if it meant spending time or lavishing affection on one or more of them. Pastor Brown taught that "everybody" is a child of God.

So Ruthie, in her distress, visited "Plain Jane's" plain church. They didn't have much in the way of singing, praise dancing, miming, or anything else "modern" or "up-to-date" that Ruthie could see. There were no well-known people in the pews. The emphasis was placed on preaching and teaching.

For Ruthie, it was almost as if she were hearing the Gospel for the first time. She repented, readily gave her life to Christ, and was baptized as a born-again believer.

Ruthie even found herself confessing and testifying publicly. This was the one act that she previously detested in the "sanctified" church. She told the church about how she partied in high school and settled down with Rick in college (nearly co-habitating).

She confessed not only to the abortion, but also to several other sins (concerning her parents) that not even Irma Jane knew about. As Irma Jane sat listening to Ruthie, tears rolled down her face.

She knew that her friend had been touched by God. They were now members of the same spiritual family. Soon, Irma Jane had something else she wanted to share with Ruthie. It was something that her pastor, Pastor Nelson, told her years earlier. Listen as she shares it in her own words.

"Ruthie, I am so thankful that the Lord has saved you. I am also thankful that He gave you the strength to leave Greater Solid Rock. Ruthie, 2nd Pentecostal is a great place with great people – the laity and the leaders alike. But even here, you will have your challenges. Not everybody here is committed to the things of God."

"Of course they may look committed. They may even act committed. Yet, there is evil here too, just as there is at Greater Solid Rock. It may not be apparent at first, but it is. This is the great mystery of iniquity, but also the mystery of godliness; they grow side-by-side closely – like wheat and tares. Ruthie, your job is to grow in godliness –regardless to what others are doing. Remember, everybody's heart has a history."

This discussion took place nearly two weeks ago. Ruthie remembered it because Ron, whom she *thought* was a "good, saved, married, brother," propositioned her. Ruthie was speechless.

Ron was exactly the type of man that Ruthie would have fallen head over heels in love with in the past. In fact, before she made a commitment to God, it would not have mattered to Ruthie whether Ron was married or not.

With his deep, soulful, voice and cool swagger, Ron appealed to every part of Ruthie. She especially liked his southern drawl and the way that he licked his lips occasionally when he talked. It was almost like she was talking to her beloved Rick – all over again.

Irma Jean warned Ruthie that Ron was adept at taking an interest in ladies who had histories of sexual immorality and being hurt by men. Irma Jean called it the "Messiah Complex."

Ron saw himself as having all the qualities that women look for in a man: he devotes time, he spares no expense, and he definitely has the looks.

"He appeals to your heart," Ruthie said, "because he knows your heart has a history."

QUESTIONS – LESSON #4

"THE HISTORY OF YOUR HEART"

"Keep thy heart with all diligence; for out of it are the issues of life." Proverbs 4:23

1. When Ruthie was a member of Greater Solid Rock, was she a committed Christian? Why or why not?

    _____

    _____

    _____

    _____

    _____

2. If good and evil, committed and uncommitted are present at every church, then was it necessary for Ruthie to change churches? Why or why not?

_____

_____

_____

_____

_____

3. In your opinion, does Ron have a healthy relationship with the Lord? Why or why not?

_____

_____

_____

_____

4. What part do you believe churches play in fostering healthy relationships?

_____

_____

_____

_____

_____

5. Has Ruthie's past made her susceptible to Ron's charms? Why or why not?

_____

_____

_____

_____

_____

6. Do you believe Ruthie's confession has made her more or less ready for marriage? Explain your thoughts.

_____

_____

_____

_____

_____

7. How do you believe Ruthie will respond to Ron's advances? Share your thoughts below.

_____

_____

_____

_____

8. Have you been involved in a relationship in which you were hurt? If so, how do you know that you have gotten over it? How much time did you give yourself before you met someone else?

_____

_____

_____

_____

9. Did you grow up in a home with both of your parents? If not, have you noticed any affect that the absence of one or both parents has had on your relationships?

_____

_____

_____

_____

_____

10. Have you ever had a person of the opposite sex try to "save you" as Ron attempted with Ruthie? If so, how did it work out?

_____

_____

_____

_____

_____

Lesson #5

"Singleness Matters"

"I wish that all men were as I am. But each man has his own gift from God; one has this gift, another has that." 1st Corinthians 7:7

For a long time, singleness has been looked upon as some sort of a social disease. Privately, men view women who have no mate as having something wrong with them.

In response, many women have tied their self-worth, self-esteem and self-appraisal to being married. The goal of most single groups, in church and elsewhere, has been to *"get married."* This has been a cultural norm for a long time.

For centuries, women have been raised, groomed, and educated to serve primarily as someone's wife. This standard was, and continues to be in some quarters, the penultimate of womanhood.

Let me be clear, there is nothing wrong with this standard. This has been a part of God's plan from the very beginning. Yet, it is still just a *part* of the plan. God's plan also includes the very special service that is rendered to Him by those who are single.

The Most Unmarried Demographic

In our day, seven out of ten (seventy percent) of African-American women are unmarried, (e.g., widowed, divorced, separated, or never married). This is the most unmarried demographic in American life.

This is not because African-American women don't desire or have not desired to be married. There are a whole host of economic, social, emotional, and spiritual issues at play in this dynamic. For instance, for every African American male who graduates from college, two African-American women graduate.

So while women have surged into middle class economically, potential marriageable mates have lagged behind. Additionally, about one in ten African American men in their thirties are in prison. Of the men who remain, their desire is to remain single until later in life, probably due to the more than ample supply of women who are available to them.

What's Wrong with Me?

Yet, when a woman is unmarried, as the great majority of African-American women are, some of them wonder privately, *"What is wrong with me?"* Secular society (and the Church as well) has unwittingly encouraged them to view their singleness as some sort of illness or debility.

If one hair is out of place, then they are not married because she *"needs to do something about her head."* If she is darker or lighter than most other women, then the issue becomes her skin color. If she is too smart, she has to play dumb. If she is a little slow, she is considered unintelligent.

Single people are often viewed as third legs. They are seen as an intrusion at Valentine Banquets and couple's galas. They are made to feel lonely and isolated. Married people have helped perpetuate this myth.

> **Try This**
>
> ✓ **Name three perceived shortcomings of being single that you have held.**

The sick lens through which we view singleness has pushed some well-meaning and well-intentioned women into risky behaviors. Imagine the emotional turmoil of having to "man-share," or the indignity of finding out that you have been unwittingly "man-sharing."

The Clock That Keeps Ticking

Even Christian women are sent the social message that they are "less-than" and somehow "incomplete" without a man. Envision the unique pressures that single women are under as they age.

First, there are the child-bearing years. Women want to have children while they are physically able. This timetable is coded into most women's DNA. A young woman can always get married later in life, but there is only a small window for bearing children.

Women want to have children while they are young, while they have the physical resources and abilities with which to raise them. When this window closes, there is a sort of emotional death in a woman's life.

The possibility for natural born children leaves. This is an emotional milestone in a woman's life. Many women cross this threshold without ever having-had a child in the bonds of married love.

As single women age, there is another emotional death and milestone that looms as well. That is the milestone of marriage. As single women age, they realize that marriage becomes less and less likely.

Try This

✓ **Name three facts of life that are influenced by time.**

Their single counterparts, older African-American men, can always marry a younger woman. They often choose the young maid over the more experienced maiden. Yet, it is less socially acceptable for the older woman to marry a younger man.

Most of us cannot hear it, but there is a very real clock ticking in the heads of single people. As that clock ticks on, the life that they could have had, fades.

The possibility of children or even more children slowly diminishes. The idea of a husband with a great married life – including physical intimacy – also becomes less likely.

The Gift of Singleness

It is from this context of singleness, with all of its complexities and perceived shortcomings, that the Bible brings forth its greatest spiritual gifts.

I would like to share three of them with you. The first gift that God gives us is the gift of wholeness that comes through a relationship with Him.

This wholeness reaches its perfection in being single. God does not have a "family and friends" plan. We each have to meet Christ alone. Marriage does not complete a person. Marriage is not the sole joy in a person's life.

Many view singleness and celibacy negatively, because we believe that men and women cannot be complete in and of themselves. Why is it that so many of us cannot be satisfied or fulfilled with Christ alone? Singleness affords the best opportunity to live this truth.

If you attend church or elsewhere, coveting or desiring other people's marriages, then you are looking to the institution of marriage to make you whole.

If you find yourself day-dreaming about the marriages on television, watch out! The institution of marriage cannot save you or make you happy.

The Single Reason that Some Married People Are Not Happy

Some married people are not happy in marriage because they were not fulfilled, or made whole when they were single.

They, too, thought marriage was the answer. Marriage is not the answer; Christ is the answer. What most people are looking for is a cure for their desire to be constantly stimulated.

In the age in which we now live, people fear being alone (young people) and growing old alone (mature people). A young man will walk off a job without having another job; but he will not leave a woman before he has found another one. He does not want to be alone.

As Christians, we have not embraced the solitude that comes from being alone. This doesn't mean that we have to live life like hermits; rather it means taking time for solitude.

Learning Christ through Solitude

Jesus always made time to be alone with the Father. This present generation is an over-stimulated generation – TV and radio for the older generation – IPOD, IPAD, and cell-phones for the younger generation.

Very few people spend any time on the deeper things that come from silence. Most have to hear some type of noise to even sleep, such as the steady drone of a fan or air conditioner, or sounds produced by a television.

We also have to hear some type of noise to wake-up – the alarm clock or some other familiar noise. Most of all, we resist solitude – even for a single night. Yet it is through aloneness that we learn Christ.

It is through silent contemplation that we develop a relationship with God; and it is through the silent communion and fellowship with God that we grow.

We can't get a message from God or to God with constant visual and auditory stimulation. Single people have a greater receptivity to the things of God and the message of God, because there should be less "noise" to distract.

The Gift of Celibacy

The second gift that God gives the single person is the gift of celibacy. Since we were all single at some point, we should have all practiced the gift of celibacy.

Celibacy does not mean that a person has never had relations; it merely means that God is presently keeping them from having relations outside of marriage. That is a gift that comes from God.

Celibacy allows the single person to value and develop friendships over sexual liaisons. Celibate friendships or relationships are less tainted by the deceit and manipulation that so characterize relationships or even friendships that involve sex or the expectation of sex. Single people who are also celibate, see the world through a lens that is not as jaded as that of those who have never had the gift of celibacy.

Some of us have been having sexual relations for so long, without any thought of celibacy, that we see others through a sexual lens. This fact cannot be denied.

If one has never experienced a period of abstinence or celibacy, as many of us have not, then we have not learned the extent to which physical relations affect us. Unfortunately, if we don't learn this lesson when we are single, it increases the likelihood that sex will take center stage in the marriage, even over companionship, and maybe even over God. Sex, "the elephant in the room," has to be tamed.

> **Try These Tips**
>
> ✓ **List at least 5 things that make you special.**
>
> ✓ **Spend at least 20 minutes each day in silent contemplation.**
>
> ✓ **Value others for who they are rather than for how they look.**

This explains the phenomenon of older men desiring much younger women after their wives slow down a little. These men have not ever valued their wives or any other woman, besides their mother, in a non-sexual way. When the highest value in a relationship is placed on sex, companionship is severely devalued. The result is that neither party fully develops spiritually.

No Cuddle Time?

Wives, this is why your husband can't just hold you. He has never really been a woman's friend with whom he wasn't interested in becoming physical. A man who has never been celibate can only see a woman in sexual terms.

> **Try This**
>
> ✓ **List the qualities you would desire in a spouse with whom you could not have sexual relations.**
>
> ✓ **Compare these qualities with those of the spouse you actually chose.**

This, in turn, is why a woman can open up so much to another woman or even to a gay man: she knows that they are not going to pressure her about sex, and can view her in an almost non-sexual way.

Again, if we never learned the gift of celibacy when we were single, sex will always take center stage in a relationship –married or otherwise. The "urge to merge" is just that strong.

It is only through celibacy that we learn to value friendship and to really see people for who they are – *aside* from their sexual proclivities.

How many of us have had good, God-honoring, enduring friendships with the opposite sex that were not tainted? It is only possible through the oversight of the Church and the gift that God provides through celibacy.

The Gift of Special Service

The third gift that God gives the single person, is the gift of special service. This is the service that the single person can perform better than most married people. Paul writes in 1st Corinthians 7:32 that "*he that is unmarried careth for the things that belong to the Lord, how he may please the Lord.*"

On the other hand, he writes in verse 33: "*But he that is married careth for the things that are of the world, how he may please his wife.*" It is not wrong to be married, but Paul says that the single person has a special service that he or she can render to the Lord.

Paul continues in verse 34 where he writes: "*The unmarried woman careth for the things of the Lord, that she may be holy both in body and in spirit: but she that is married careth for the things of the world, how she may please her husband.*"

The married person has a host of obligations. The single person is truly free to serve the Lord at a level that a married person oftentimes cannot. Pastorally, I can call a Deacon, whose wife is deceased, at any time of the day or night. I will call on him at odd hours before I will disturb another Deacon, who has been to work and has not spent any time with his wife and children.

For those of you who are single, celibate and desiring to serve the Lord, you ought to ask Him, "*Lord, what is my special service to you?*" The gift of being single is for single-minded service and devotion to the things of God.

Make no mistake about it, what we practice in a life of singleness often follows us into marriage. It may even be said that the life we lived when we were single, serves as the foundation for our later years, married or otherwise.

Illustration 5-1

Meet the Wife – Jane

Outwardly Jane is
Tall, Beautiful, Talented

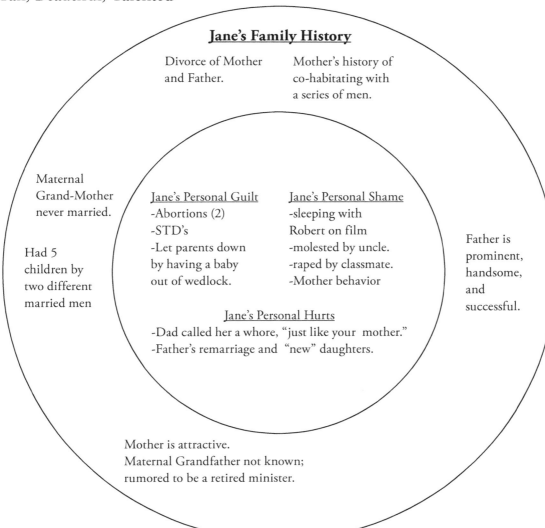

Jane's Family History

Divorce of Mother and Father.

Mother's history of co-habitating with a series of men.

Maternal Grand-Mother never married.

Had 5 children by two different married men

Jane's Personal Guilt
-Abortions (2)
-STD's
-Let parents down by having a baby out of wedlock.

Jane's Personal Shame
-sleeping with Robert on film
-molested by uncle.
-raped by classmate.
-Mother behavior

Jane's Personal Hurts
-Dad called her a whore, "just like your mother."
-Father's remarriage and "new" daughters.

Father is prominent, handsome, and successful.

Mother is attractive.
Maternal Grandfather not known; rumored to be a retired minister.

Illustration 5-2

Meet the Husband – John

Outwardly John is:
Hardworking, Ambitious

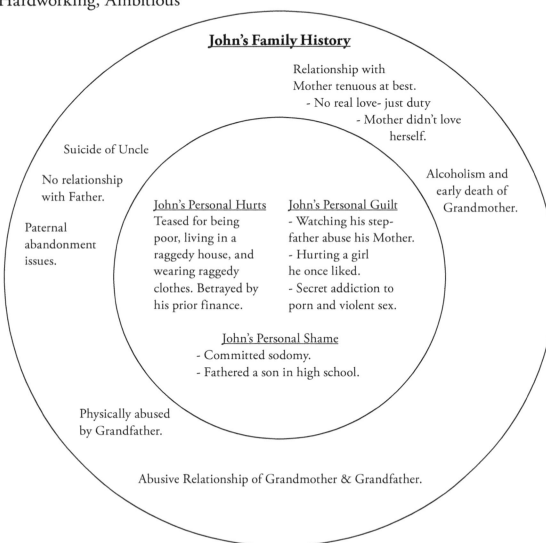

John's Family History

Relationship with
Mother tenuous at best.
  - No real love- just duty
    - Mother didn't love
      herself.

Suicide of Uncle

No relationship
with Father.

Alcoholism and
early death of
Grandmother.

Paternal
abandonment
issues.

John's Personal Hurts
Teased for being
poor, living in a
raggedy house, and
wearing raggedy
clothes. Betrayed by
his prior finance.

John's Personal Guilt
- Watching his step-
father abuse his Mother.
- Hurting a girl
he once liked.
- Secret addiction to
porn and violent sex.

John's Personal Shame
- Committed sodomy.
- Fathered a son in high school.

Physically abused
by Grandfather.

Abusive Relationship of Grandmother & Grandfather.

CASE STUDY – LESSON #5

"SINGLENESS MATTERS"

"I wish that all men were as I am. But each man has his own gift from God; one has this gift, another has that." 1st Corinthians 7:7

"Not again!" Jane thought. *"Why does this keep happening to me! Why do men keep treating me this way! Uughh!"* Jane had only known Robert for six weeks or so, but it was evident that their "relationship" was over. She was in her dorm room crying, with her roommate and best friend, Emma Granger.

What turned out to be a simple birthday request from a boyfriend to his girlfriend, had turned into another nightmare. This one was really bad. Jane even thought about killing herself. *"What's wrong with me?"* she thought. *"I'm pretty. I'm smart. I give good love."*

Jane allowed their last love-making session, on Robert's birthday, to be filmed. She had an elaborate plan for the evening of his birthday. He spent the day with some of his fraternity brothers, but he promised to spend the night with Jane. She thought the night was best anyway!

What a night it would be! Jane had everything planned, down to the color of the under-garments that she wore – purple and gold for Robert's fraternity. Robert was running late as usual, and when he arrived, he had a video-recorder that he said was a birthday gift from a friend.

He wanted to film every moment of what he said would be a "night to remember." Always accommodating, Jane acquiesced and slipped into her role as dutiful girlfriend. She really wanted Robert to know how much she loved him!

She poured her passion into him, and he graciously accepted. Jane left thinking, *he will always remember me.* Little did she know that Robert had already forgotten her – long before the night began.

The names had changed, but the story remained the same: a man proved he didn't care anything about Jane. Robert showed the film to his friends and refused to accept any of her calls. In six months, he would be married to someone else that he barely knew.

Jane's best friend, Emma, told her that Robert would never marry a girl who already had a child (which Jane did), or who had "slept around" (as Jane also did). But as usual, Jane knew better. She said her past didn't matter to Robert. Emma was always reminding her of things that she would rather forget, like the secret trips to have abortions and the couple of times she had to be treated for STDs.

"Slow down," Emma said, "allow yourself to heal from the past. What you have done when you are single, matters when you get married."

"No, Emma, this is college. This is what college is supposed to be like," Jane responded. "We all make mistakes, right?"

All Jane knew was how she felt when Robert looked at her. He didn't see the past. All he saw was her. Robert made her feel "needed." All that other stuff was in the past now. Robert was so handsome, just like her father. He was smart, too! Who knows, maybe she was going to be Mrs. Robert Jackson! The next weeks' events proved that this was definitely not to be the case.

Another rape, Jane thought as she recalled how she was raped her freshman year. No one believed her then as a naïve young lady, and she didn't bother to mention to anyone what was happening to her now. She just wanted to graduate and get this embarrassing chapter of her life behind her.

Soon Briarcliff College and Savannah, Georgia, were distant memories. After graduation, Jane relocated to Smithville, Arkansas. She had accepted a job as a Staff Accountant with Bakersfield Brands.

Despite her somewhat dark and dubious past, Jane was definitely going to make something of herself professionally and socially. She would not content herself with a life that didn't include marriage and stability.

She had experienced too much instability, after her mother and father divorced when she was just 3 years old. No, Jane would not settle for just "a man," she wanted a "husband" and a father for little Carolyn. Ever since her parents divorced and Jane suffered through a series of "daddies" and "uncles," she promised herself that she would do better than her mother, as far as men were concerned.

Emma, ever the prophet, said that Jane had to be careful because "singleness" and "promiscuity" seemed to run in Jane's family. She may have even quoted a Bible verse or two. Exodus 20:5…as Jane remembered…something about being born out of wedlock and generational curses. That Emma was too much into morality! She didn't know how to let church stay at the Church. Didn't God give people second chances?

Emma, who had known Jane since she was six, was making reference to Jane's maternal grandmother, who never married, but had several children, including, of course, Jane's mother. More than once over the years, Emma had also impeached the character of Jane's mother, Sarah, hinting that she was not good marriage material to begin with.

Since everybody seemed to lack faith in *her* marriageability; marriage was Jane's dream and goal. She had something to prove to her mother. "I am not my mother," she had told Emma more than once. It wasn't her fault that the men she dated couldn't see how special she is. Jane also worked extra hard to be successful professionally, like her father.

She really wanted to follow in his footsteps and make him proud in so many ways. To hear Jane talk, one would have thought that she had a perfectly "normal" relationship with her father, but that definitely was not the case. Jane's father, the much esteemed medical doctor, Stafford Vincent, was quite the success story.

So successful was he that he no longer mentioned that he had a "first" wife and a "first" daughter. Of course, the substantial child support came over the years, but Dr. Vincent didn't. It seems that he wished to forget, or more accurately, had forgotten not only his first wife, but Jane as well.

Once old enough, Jane had kept up with him through social media and various professional publications. She dared not contact him. His life was already perfect – if not complete.

He had a loving wife and two teenage daughters. Her sisters, she thought. They lived in an exclusive community, and his daughters attended the best schools. Although they lived in the same city, they were worlds apart. Jane was determined to make a name for herself and build a life that would be the envy of her parents.

She had made a good start in Bakersfield Brands. Bakersfield was the nation's second-largest producer of snack cakes. Its name was well known. Emma attributed Jane's hiring as "an act of God," while Jane said there was nothing that her good looks and determination could not handle.

Six months on the job, and Jane had forgotten Robert and her last semester in Savannah. Life was a lot slower in Smithville. Not that Jane had a chance to indulge in any of the night life, though.

She was too exhausted after training sessions, trips to Corporate in Washington, D.C., and learning all of the little general ledger and trial balance tricks that made one a successful Staff Accountant at Bakersfield Brands. For once, Jane was not distracted with a relationship. She missed Emma, she was even looking for a church home, that is, until she met John Mahoney, CPA.

John, just a few years older than Jane, was the Plant Controller in Smithville. His meteoric rise was the lore of Bakersfield Brands. Jane had been scheduled to meet with John when she was interviewing. Even then, she had heard that he had such a presence about him.

She was not the least bit surprised when she discovered that John had been called away to Corporate for an emergency meeting and could not interview her. There were talks of a merger with Cisco Brands, the nation's third largest snack food provider.

Certainly Bakersfield would need one of its brightest financial stars to help lead the way! In fact, for most of her first six months in Smithville, John was back and forth to Corporate headquarters so much that she surmised, correctly, that he was being promoted again.

John was so ambitious, Jane thought. When she finally met him, she was smitten! It was as if she were meeting her soul-mate. There was something so familiar about him!

They had only been in the conference room together for ten minutes before both of them were smitten. She could see the lonely look in his eyes. Yes, he wanted her, no *needed* her, just as badly as she *needed* him. Within the year, they were married and had relocated to Corporate.

Their marriage was easy at first – almost like a dream come true. It was all about Bakersfield Brands during the day and newly-wedded bliss each night! There were trips all over the U.S. for business purposes during which they managed to work in a whole lot of pleasure as well.

They were indeed "*living the life*." Emma, ever the realist, called it "*living the lie*." She correctly pointed out that John and Jane barely knew one another and that the baggage from their individual lives, especially of that immediately preceding the marriage, would soon surface. She would always ask Jane:

"Where does this man have a track record of acknowledging God? What was he like when he was single? Who did he date before he met you? Were they celibate? What was his home life like as a child? What does he do for fun and why is he so driven?"

Emma believed that a marriage had to be based on more than just "feelings." A personal devotion to God had to be at the center.

"Em," as Jane liked to call her, "you're not the only one who has attended church. Why do you always have to be so pessimistic? Why can't you be happy for me just this once?"

"Jane, I am happy, but I can't sit back and watch the adult version of what has been happening to you all of your life without saying anything," Emma replied. "You have never really put God first. You have always desired intimacy from men, but without godly intimacy, your marriage will always lack a spiritual component."

"Em, how can you say that?" Jane quickly retorted. "John and I do have a spiritual connection. Can't you see it? We are soul mates!"

"No, Jane. You are both lost without God, and soon, you will both be married and lonely. Neither of you can continue at this torrid pace. You barely spend any meaningful time together, and both of your lives are centered around Bakersfield Brands."

"What you feel for John is not love. It is the unconscious attraction of people who have similar backgrounds. Yes, he *is* just like you. That is why you need to be cautious and find out more about him. He probably has a kid stuck somewhere, just like you have Carolyn back at home with your mother. Both of your hearts have a history, and you need to share them. What you did when you were single matters in your marriage."

It was another stinging rebuke. Jane thought she had finally gained an air of respectability by becoming the prestigious, Mrs. John Mahoney, CPA. The very name seemed to carry with it the aura of success and stability, much like the name Mrs. Stafford Vincent, MD.

Although Jane and John were not as established as Dr. and Mrs. Stafford Vincent, they were well on their way. That is, until John hit a roadblock in his career. Emma's words proved to be prophetic.

John had been brought to D.C. under the assumption that he was being groomed for the job of the soon to be retiring Chief Financial Officer. This was John's dream job. Ever since he took a double-entry bookkeeping class in high school, it had been his dream to be the CFO of a Fortune 500 company.

John, much like Jane, had come from a background of degradation and neglect. Born in inner city, Ohio, the son of a single parent, John was raised in the harshest of environments. He never knew his father and had an adversarial relationship with his step-father, who mercilessly beat his mother and had also physically abused John on more than one occasion.

John hated home and especially resented his mother for exposing him to a life of abuse. He often imagined that his real father had to be somebody important who would one day be proud of him.

School seemed to be John's only way out. Shorter and less physically gifted than most other kids in his neighborhood, athletics were out of the question. However, John seemed to have a knack and a natural proclivity for numbers. Perhaps, it was due to his tendency to reduce almost everything to how much it costs.

John could compute every bill that he brought in from the mailbox and determine how much money was needed for that month. He could also quickly determine how much money his mother had to have in the check-out line at the grocery store.

Even with a mind as naturally gifted for numbers as his, John felt like he had to constantly prove himself. It was as if the mind that he possessed was incompatible with his well-worn clothes and tattered shoes.

John was constantly teased by those who didn't know him, for being just another nameless, faceless, student from the poorest side of town. But to those who knew him, John was full of ambition and a genius with numbers. Indeed, John Mahoney wanted to make a name for himself.

Socially, however, John was a bit awkward. He had already been exposed to sex of the sickest kind through the paper-thin walls of the various houses his mother rented over the years.

Not one for the social niceties of the female variety, John spent most of his time with boys and young men of his own age – most of whom had tumultuous family histories, similar to his.

Like most of them, he engaged in many senseless acts of sexual depravity. By the time he was a senior in college, he had already fathered one child, that he knew for certain, but there could be others.

John was very "cold" emotionally. He didn't feel anything for his child nor his child's mother. In fact, John didn't allow himself to feel anything for his own mother. Of course, he was always respectful and courteous; but underneath, he was usually seething with contempt.

John liked numbers because they were devoid of any feeling or comprehension. They just existed. They were the facts. What could not be seen or computed could not be known.

This was also the way that John felt about God. "If there is a god, certainly he can't be known." John dealt with the opposite sex in much the same matter-of-fact way. With John, it had always been, "the facts don't lie."

This was why John took the loss of the CFO position so hard. The facts said that he should be the CFO, but the CEO used a number against him – his age.

"John, you're just too young," the CEO said. "We value your hard work and dedication. We just need more experience in this position. That is why I am promoting the CFO of Cisco Brands, Tyler Bracken, to be the CFO of the combined company."

John was crushed. All of a sudden his meteoric career was found to have a ceiling. When his career hit that ceiling, the roof caved in at home. The normally reserved John was now outright cold toward his bride of two years.

Jane had thought that with less travel and overtime that they would enjoy spending more time in their new home. This was not the case. John began to find Jane incredibly annoying.

"You worry about things that are not worth worrying about," John had said more than once to Jane.

In John's way of thinking, Jane was also spending too much money – especially for a person who never really had a lot of money. Jane was tall and beautiful; she had to be attracted to him for the money.

John remembered the way that Jane always looked at him when he was on his way up in the company. It was a look of pure, materialistic, adoration. John thought, *She doesn't love me. Just like all women, she loves the ride.*

John was thinking about Cindy, his former fiancée, who broke off their engagement to marry an engineering student, because he had "better future earning potential." He was also thinking about his mother and how she would be secretly happy to know that he had finally failed.

Jane saw in John a person who seemed to be rather bitter all of a sudden, and one who looked down upon her as an object rather than a person. What he used to see in her and love, he now loathed. At least that is the way Jane felt.

It was obvious to Jane that John needed some professional help. His mind and his thinking were definitely twisted.

"Has he always been this way?" she wondered aloud one morning. "I feel like I don't even know this man. Who can even reach him?"

Soon, at Emma's insistence, Jane began to attend a Bible study group for married ladies.

Questions – Lesson #5

"Singleness Matters"

"I wish that all men were as I am. But each man has his own gift from God; one has this gift, another has that." 1st Corinthians 7:7

1. In your opinion, will Jane and John's marriage survive? Why or why not?

   _____
   _____
   _____
   _____
   _____

2. What impact has the past had on their marriage? Be detailed from the facts given.

   _____
   _____
   _____
   _____
   _____

3. Without God, is there a common thread that can hold this marriage together?

   _____
   _____
   _____
   _____
   _____

4. Based on the information in Lesson #2, "The Little Things" what are some of the common failings of Jane and John?

   _____
   _____
   _____
   _____

5. Emma accused Jane and John of heading toward being "Married and Lonely." Based on the information in Lesson #3, "Busy Days and Lonely Nights," how could this be true?

_____

_____

_____

_____

_____

6. How do you believe the past significant relationships of Jane and John have affected their marriage? The information in Lesson #4, "The History of Your Heart," may be useful in answering this question.

_____

_____

_____

_____

_____

7. What are the signs that John and/or Jane may need some intervention? Are married couples forthright enough to know when professional help may be necessary? Consider some of the ideas explained in Lesson #7, "Professional Help."

_____

_____

_____

_____

_____

8. What are some common mistakes that single people make that usually hinder them in marriage? Consider some of the ideas pointed out in this lesson.

_____

_____

_____

_____

_____

9. Does a marriage benefit from partners who were celibate before marriage? Why or why not?

_____

_____

_____

_____

_____

10. If a person remains celibate prior to marriage, do you believe that God will reward them in marriage?

_____

_____

_____

_____

_____

Lesson #6

"Seasoned and Satisfied"

"I have learned in whatsoever state I am, therewith to be content." Philippians 4:11

Some of the more severe trials of life, come as we age. We all burst forth in life with the exuberance that accompanies youth. But as we age, the idealism of youth ultimately gives way to the realism of old age.

The experience gained through the harsh reality of living, then being faced with the prospect of an impending death, brings about the special temptation, near the end of one's life, of feeling cheated by life itself.

Issues Facing An Aging Generation

The issues facing an aging generation are many. Perhaps the most significant, is the one that goes generally unnoticed. The older we become, quite naturally, the less time we have left to "get it right."

As an aging person looks back over his or her life, sometimes there is the feeling of extreme dissatisfaction with one's life as a whole. It is the feeling that things are not as good as they could be, and that they may not get any better because time is running out. The result is an extreme dissatisfaction with life itself.

This dissatisfaction as we age is manifested through the meanness, pettiness, jealousy, and utter childishness that is exhibited by the person who is aging, and yet, who feels somehow cheated by life. This less than mellow persona tends to color the remainder of this person's life.

So common is this psychological phenomenon, that youngsters often view their grandparents as old, crotchety and quite often downright mean. Marriages that were rock-solid earlier in life, later are on sinking sand because one party feels cheated by life.

Single Seniors

Those seniors who are single, sometimes end up in behaviors that are unbefitting of a person of their age and experience. Single grandmothers become "cougars," and single grandfathers become "dirty old men."

When the music is turned down enough, and when the television, cell phone and Facebook are turned off; the life that seems to others to be so exciting "for an older person," is really one of quiet despair.

Some older people act out of character in their interactions with others simply because they feel cheated. They never envisioned this final stage of their lives being what it is. In fact, many were of the opinion that life would just keep getting better and better. Retirement was viewed as the ultimate goal. As is so often the case in life, the reality of retirement is nowhere near as exciting as it looked years before.

Let's begin by using a younger lady as an example. When women are younger they don't contemplate the physical changes that lie ahead of them: wrinkles, sagging skin and perhaps children and grandchildren who will one day no longer need them.

Menopause and Beyond

Younger women don't contemplate the physiological and psychological effects of menopause – which they will all experience if they live long enough. Most women have always seen themselves as "desirable."

Yet the day will most certainly come when most men will not give them a second look. Sometimes, even their own husbands, who are physically able to be intimate, will also pull away from them. It is enough to make a woman feel cheated if she has not come to terms with the passing years and the changes that they bring.

What this now older woman doesn't realize, is that this sense of being "cheated" by life is exactly what makes her undesirable to her husband. She has succumbed to this special temptation for seniors. I like to call it the "Senior Citizen's Special."

Senior Women, Try This

✓ **Each year, take a Biblical passage, (e.g., Titus 2:3-5) and focus on developing each virtue.**

Time and circumstance cause us to doubt that our lives mean anything. Dissatisfaction keeps us looking back on what we lacked in life, rather than looking forward, ultimately to our union with Christ.

Continuing with our example, when a woman looks back, she is filled with a sense of being cheated: *the children did this to me,* *my husband did that to me,* *I regret that I didn't do this,* and *I regret that I didn't do that.*

Cheated by God?

Our lives are not just about "us." When we make our lives solely about "us," that is a good sign of a woman who feels cheated by God. Paul called this attitude "godless" and "thankless" in Romans 1:21.

As we age, there ought to be a growing attitude of gratefulness to God. Shouldn't we be more appreciative of the gift of longevity? After all, does life really owe us anything? My friend, you can only be cheated when you are owed something.

If life were a card game, some senior citizens would be upset with God because He is the dealer, and they don't like the hand they were given. Some are not satisfied with *anything* about their lives, even though God has blessed them with five, six, or even seven decades of life to work out some of these negative feelings.

So many are threatening to ruin their lives near the very end by not coming to accept some universal truths about life.

At the Mount of Olives, Jesus could have ruined God's plan to redeem mankind at the very end by refusing to accept God's plan. Jesus confessed that the cup set before Him was indeed bitter, but He desired to do God's will rather than His own.

> **Try These Tips**
>
> ✓ **Ask your spouse to name one thing that would make you a better spouse.**
>
> ✓ **Ask your spouse how he or she defines "love."**
>
> ✓ **Compile a list of things for which you are grateful.**

Contrary to popular belief, confession is good. It helps us accept some ugly truths about our lives. That is why we look back, when we do. We look back to confess that what we did, and perhaps what some others did, was not always right. Then, perhaps, we can accept what happened and move forward.

Grumpy Old Men

The feeling of being cheated as we age, doesn't escape the men either. For instance, at every stage of a sexually immoral man's life, he defines how he relates to women and especially his wife in sexual terms.

As these men age, God will sometimes take the very thing that a man has defined himself by for so many years. Most of the time He does this through the prostate. If you want to see a mean man, observe one who has had his prostate removed and hasn't come to grips with it. I have seen it in years past.

A man who was nice and cordial earlier in life, will sometimes begin to lash out at his wife and everyone else around him later in life. His circumstances are now somebody else's fault.

A young man's jealousy is easily aroused when it comes to his new bride; but you haven't truly witnessed jealousy, until you witness an older man accuse his wife of adultery.

He has had the Senior Citizen's Special served up to him. He is checking the odometer on her car to determine the truthfulness of where she has been. His wife has to call him each time she is away from him.

> **Senior Men, Try This**
>
> ✓ **Ask your wife or daughter how has your personality changed over the years.**
>
> ✓ **Find an older man that you admire to mentor you as you age.**

In a minority of cases, he speaks to her in a way that is morally shameful. His mind, as it pertains to his marriage, is literally messed up. He is defending his aging manhood when it doesn't need defending.

Men Who Have Gone through the Change

Age, and the diminution of a man's physical powers, sometimes make him paranoid. Believe it, some women can't go to the store to purchase a carton of milk. Every man that passes, she has to hold her head down simply because her husband may have one of his "peculiar" thoughts about his wife, and this man that she doesn't know. The man who does this is destroying his marriage and not trusting God.

Many men have it planted in their heads that women just have to have "relations," even when it should be obvious they don't. This type of thinking is the spiritual harvest of a legacy of sexual immorality. The seeds were planted years ago, and are full grown by the time these men are in their sixties.

A woman is generally going through menopause and one of the absolute last things on her mind is "relations;" yet, the man with a long history of sexual immorality can't stop thinking about "relations," even though he can't perform nearly as regularly as he once did.

Sadly, he assumes that if his wife, especially in the case of couples who married later in life, is not active with him, she is active with somebody, anybody!

This is what he has believed about women all of his life. He feels cheated! The question may naturally arise, "Where is God in all of this?"

Where Is God?

The passage of time and its effects on the human body and mind should cause Christians to trust God even more. God can be trusted even and especially as we age.

At the end of this life, if God allows us to live long enough, everything is going to fail. Everything about our bodies will give out. God made it that way. He has another body for us – a heavenly body (1st Corinthians 15:53).

Decline in one's physical capabilities is natural (1st Corinthians 15:50). It is also natural that as one's physical capabilities diminish, our hope in Christ should be strengthening. In the end, everything else will fail, except our relationship with Him.

Try This

....

✓ **Make a list of relationships in your life that you would like to see strengthened.**

✓ **Work on strengthening the relationships you listed.**

Perhaps Paul put it best in Colossians 3:2-4: "*Set your affection on things above, not on things on the earth. For ye are dead, and your life is hid with Christ in God. When Christ, who is our life, shall appear, then shall ye also appear with him in glory.*"

When faced with life's inherent limitations, whether married, widowed, divorced or single, remember Paul's rhetorical, yet, eternal question: "*Who shall separate us from the love of Christ?*" This is the mark of the seasoned and satisfied saint!

Case Study – Lesson #6

"Seasoned and Satisfied"

"I have learned in whatsoever state I am, therewith to be content." Philippians 4:11

Elijah and Sarah – "Sweet or Sour?"

"God wants to grow Christians – not wide – but deep!" thundered the plain-spoken, Baptist preacher dressed in a simple black robe. *"Too many Christians are of the 'sweet and sour' variety: when things are going well for them, they are sweet, but when things are not going so well, they are sour!"*

Reverend Brown is really preaching today, thought Sarah. *I wonder is Elijah listening?*

Sarah almost got carried away in her quiet reverie until she heard the Pastor say: "*Rather than act like we are 'spiritually bipolar' – one day we're happy and the next day we are sad – God calls Christians to have joy. Joy is not like happiness. Happiness is ephemeral and fleeting. Joy is eternal!*"

Sarah could have shouted! She and her husband Elijah should have been on an extended honeymoon – they had only been married 3 years – but with the distance between them, it felt more like thirty-three. Yes, they were both up in age, not quite seventy, but close, they were sixty-seven.

Still, there was so much life left to live! They were both in relatively good health, and they were both retired with lots of time on their hands. But one quick glance to her left and Sarah saw that Elijah, a church elder, was sleep again! No matter how much sleep he got at night, these short bouts with sleep would catch him anytime he sat down longer than five minutes.

Sarah really needed Elijah to hear this message. It was almost like the preacher had been in their house, or to be more exact, reading her thoughts! So she gently nudged Elijah, as she so often did when he fell asleep in church. The church was nearly raucous. *How could he sleep through this?* Sarah thought. Almost on cue, Elijah awoke and sheepishly nodded his head to the preacher and said, "*A-men.*"

Reverend Brown was really preaching now! "*Sour people live to be happy. If it's not new; if they can't brag about it; if it's not better than yours; if it's not going their way; then they are not happy.*"

"*Preach on, Brother!*" Sarah heard someone shout. Looks like the Reverend was planning on doing just that!

"*Sour people pretend for a while, but eventually it comes out. 'I'm just not happy.' These are also the people who want to be 'in love,' but who don't know how to truly love. They equate being 'in love' with happiness. This type of love entails no responsibility.*"

Even those who normally praised the Pastor for his diction and erudition, today seemed to be more focused on the content of his message.

"Sour people live merely for the good times, the accolades, and the pats on the back. When they are not getting that, they are sour. Sourness has a way of affecting everybody around us. When we are negative, we suck the life out of everybody around us."

Elijah, who had his prostate removed just last year, seemed to change after the surgery. To use Reverend Brown's terminology, Elijah had "soured." The joy was gone. The normally jovial, good-natured, lovable, and yes, handsome, man that she met was now a distant and fading memory. Sure, he would flash his old trademark smile from time to time, but he just wasn't the same.

Elijah didn't even look the same. He looked like an old man! His mood had definitely darkened. No matter what Sarah did to appease him, even jokingly calling him 'lord,' just like her namesake in 1st Peter 3:6, Elijah still responded dryly. He wasn't openly hostile, but his outlook on life had definitely changed for the worse; as a result, their marriage had changed for the worse.

That's why this message today is definitely hitting home. Sarah didn't want the very pointed preaching to end. The normally staid Reverend Brown seemed happy to oblige!

"Sour people try to bring you down. They want you to be sour. They want to point out other people's faults to you; so that you can start complaining. They live to give you bad news, or to give you a hard time."

"They can't help it, because they don't understand your joy. They look around for a tangible reason for why you should be so joyous. You can have sweet and sour living in the same house as husband and wife. One is always carping and complaining that they are not happy because they don't have 'this' or 'that'; but the other is always trusting God."

Sarah couldn't tell what Elijah was thinking. He was on his feet encouraging the Pastor to "Preach!" but that was just his church routine.

Probably all out of habit, Sarah thought. Lately, it was as if he believed all women were evil.

Elijah constantly accused, harassed, harangued, and otherwise made her life miserable – especially if she had been away from him during the day. What did he think a sixty-seven-year-old, saved woman would be doing? What was next, a divorce, at their age?

It sounded strange just thinking about it, but they had no children together or any other significant tie that would keep them together. Secretly, Sarah felt like it would almost be a relief to Elijah if she did leave. As if still on cue, Reverend Brown belted out the following words:

"People with no joy, feel like they have no security. That's right, people who may have experienced some setbacks in their lives, don't perceive any security in their lives."

"They perceive God as being so random: sometimes He's good to them and sometimes He's not. Then too, folks who have been hurt in the past need to see some security before they will allow themselves to be happy."

Sarah had always heard about men who had gone "through the change." Somehow when the desire for physical intimacy, or even the physical energies of some men waned, the more possessive and controlling they become. Sometimes she felt like Elijah was struggling, trying to hold on to his manhood.

When contemplating the prostate surgery, Sarah never thought Elijah would become that way. Their intimacy prior to the surgery was regular, predictable, and loving – almost like the character of the man she married.

Although their physical intimacy was now non-existent, it didn't bother Sarah. Sarah had been celibate for years after the death of her first husband. Elijah pretended that this period of 'celibacy in marriage' didn't bother him, but he seemed to be bitterly disappointed about everything else in the marriage.

Perhaps Elijah's sour moods would have affected the attitudes of younger women, but Sarah was determined that this would not be her! She shouted for joy as she heard Reverend Brown's closing words:

"Joy, on the other hand, is when our hope and our security is placed firmly in Christ. His salvation becomes the main reason that we have to be joyous."

"Joy differs from happiness because the believer can never be separated from Christ. Said simply, nobody can ever take your joy. Paul asked in Romans 8:35 in the NLT: 'Can anything ever separate us from the love of Christ?'"

As Sarah made her way to the altar, she didn't turn back to see if Elijah followed.

Questions – Lesson #6

"Seasoned and Satisfied"

"I have learned in whatsoever state I am, therewith to be content." Philippians 4:11

1. Why do you believe Sarah went to the altar?

   _____

   _____

   _____

   _____

   _____

2. Do you agree that some people age badly in terms of their outlook on life? Why or why not? If so, to what do you attribute this phenomenon?

   _____

   _____

   _____

   _____

   _____

3. Do you believe that Elijah's outlook would be different if he and Sarah had been married for thirty years or more? Why or why not?

   _____

   _____

   _____

   _____

   _____

4. Do you believe that prolonged periods of sexual immorality early in life have a psychological effect later in life? If so, why?

   _____

   _____

   _____

   _____

5. Based on the information provided in Lesson #6, "Seasoned Saints," what are some of the differences in trusting God through the various stages and seasons of an individual life?

_____

_____

_____

_____

_____

6. Do you believe Elijah followed his wife to the altar? Why or why not?

_____

_____

_____

_____

_____

7. List some of the stages of life that a woman goes through as she ages. For each stage you list, also list the probable effect on her marriage.

_____

_____

_____

_____

_____

8. List some of the stages of life that a man goes through as he ages. For each stage you list, also list the probable effect on his marriage.

_____

_____

_____

_____

_____

9. When medical procedures are performed later in life, on us or our spouses, should we also contemplate the psychological changes that may occur, in addition to the physiological ones? Why or why not?

_____

_____

_____

_____

_____

10. Name a few ways that marital trust should strengthen as couples age.

_____

_____

_____

_____

_____

Lesson #7

"Professional Help"

"Wilt thou be made whole?" John 5:6

The man at the pool needed help. He didn't just start needing help. This man had an infirmity for thirty-eight long years. While the infirmity did not kill him, it did severely limit his enjoyment of life.

The man had been limited for so long that his mind was no longer on the ultimate remedy, which was to be made whole by getting in the pool when the water was troubled; rather, his mind was now set on finding somebody to put him in the pool. The man at the pool, described in John 5:1-9, needed help.

When Spiritual Sicknesses Become Normal

Understand that so many of us have been so spiritually sick for so long, that our sicknesses have, of a necessity, become "normal" to us. Less than friendly attitudes are "normal." Not speaking in the morning is now "normal." Thinking bad thoughts is "normal."

Many of us have been sick for so long that we have just learned to function with our sicknesses – even in our marriages. We have given up on a cure for what we have. *"That's just me,"* we think to ourselves.

Spiritually speaking, we need professional help. Regardless to what we think, there is another level of help that is to be had spiritually. This level of help becomes available as our thinking about our situation changes.

The man by the pool called Bethesda, or "the House of Mercy," had learned to function with his sickness just like our imaginary wife and husband, in Illustrations 5-1 and 5-2.

We all have to continue living, even though the enjoyment of our living may be limited by our mental outlook. Undoubtedly, the man would have died in that limited condition if Jesus had not traveled that way.

Where Is Your Hope?

Prior to Jesus, the man's only hope was that somebody would put him into the pool after the water was troubled. Over the course of his long illness, the man had gone from thinking in terms of "cure" to thinking in terms of "hope to make it through the day."

That was his limited mental outlook. In his mind, that was the only logical way to make it. Yet my friends, there is another way, God's true way, if you are mentally open to it. *"Well, I thought I was already doing it God's way."*

In all likelihood, you are merely functioning in light of your limitations. But just because you are limited in your thinking or in your perception, that doesn't mean that God is limited, or that God can't broaden your perspective.

Sometimes, in our own minds, we haven't really turned our troubled relationship over to Him. Perhaps you are still looking for somebody to place you (or more likely your spouse) in the pool, rather than accept the professional help that you may need.

Sometimes, the sex may be good, but everything else may be really bad. Alternatively, we may have tried the 'little things' and even sharing our 'tender grapes;' but we may still need professional help to examine the history of our own hearts. Perhaps this help comes at the hands of an experienced Christian counselor, or even through the loving oversight of a Church pastor or elder.

> **Try This**
>
> ✓ **The next time you are accused of something, take the time to view the accusations from your accuser's perspective.**

That is the essence of Jesus' question to the man. The question, *"Will thou be made whole?"* is an attempt by Jesus to take the limits or the restrictions off the man's thinking.

Notice that the man doesn't directly answer Jesus' question. If it would have been me, I would have "jumped," metaphorically speaking, at the very chance to be healed.

Stop Focusing on Limitations

But this man, for thirty-eight years, has focused on his limitation or just on making it from day to day. He doesn't immediately see total deliverance as even a viable option. He also sees his own healing as involving the pool of water. His mind never allowed him to believe that it could be any other way.

Many of us have had less than pleasing dispositions in our relationships for so long that we consider it *"who we are."* We have also structured our lives around limitations.

> **Try This**
> ✓ **Never stop believing that God can change your spouse.**

Many of us have struggled with issues of depression and self-doubt for so long that we just consider it a "normal" part of our lives. Like the man at the pool, we have settled down into our limitations.

One would think that a man who has been infirm for thirty and eight years would want nothing more than to be healed. But over the years, his thinking slowly changed from the idealism of youth, to the realism of middle age, and, finally, to his present pessimism.

So Jesus had to ask the question, and in His infinite mercy, He healed the man, even though the man didn't directly answer Him. Jesus also healed in a manner that was unexpected. The healing didn't involve the water at all.

The larger question for us, in the context of relationships, is how did the man's thinking become so limited? Within this question is the professional help that we all need.

From an anatomical and biological perspective, every stimulus in the natural world leaves an impression on the human brain. Each day of our existence is filled with thousands of stimuli that vie for our attention.

Busy, Busy, Busy

Let's take an imaginary snapshot of five minutes of your life. This could be any five minutes.

One minute the phone rings. You answer it, and then put it on vibrate. Then, there is the video you are trying to watch on Facebook. There is also the conversation that your friend wants to have to with you, and the magazine that you are busy trying to scan while pretending to listen to your friend.

In the background, you are eavesdropping on somebody else's conversation. Surprisingly, you are also picking up on all sorts of non-verbal communication all around you. Then, too, each time you hear a new sound, you look towards it.

All of these events and more can happen within five minutes. This is counting only the stimuli that reach the level of consciousness. There are all sorts of other stimuli that vie for your attention that never get it.

For instance, there is the child tugging on your sleeve, but you didn't feel the tug. You received a text message, your phone vibrated, but you didn't feel it. Somebody called your name, and you didn't hear them.

Biologists, psychologists and psychiatrists are still unraveling the mysteries of the human brain. What they do understand, is that what a person is exposed to repeatedly creates electro-chemical impressions on the brain. These electro-chemical impressions slowly alter the way that a person processes information.

To What Have You Been Exposed?

What we are repeatedly exposed to has a definite effect on us. The earlier in life that we are exposed to certain negative stimuli, the more disfiguring the effect.

Our lives are lived in the shadows of how we learned to process various events when we were younger.

If you can imagine the brain being a super-highway, then all the highways of each life are laid during the first few years of a person's life. Consider the events that shaped the lives of Jane and John in Illustrations 5-1 and 5-2, respectively.

> **Try This**
>
> ✓ **Confess to someone about how your bad thinking has caused trouble in your life.**

How does Jane process the sexual immorality of her mother or the hurtful words of her father? What effect does this have on her relationship with John? Of course, this happened years before she met John.

It is not that we can't learn anything new after we are adults; rather, the new learning is processed over the old highways. Again, the way we process information is determined very early in life by what we were repeatedly exposed to.

How did the prideful person ever become prideful? They were programmed early on to be prideful. Perhaps, mother and father raised them in a way that repeatedly encouraged them to believe that somehow they were better than others.

Those who are prideful have also had many experiences which reinforced the thought that they were somehow better than others. So, no matter what the new experience or the new situation, the prideful person processes all the information or the stimuli over a mind that is predisposed to pride.

Can You See It?

This person may never see themselves as being prideful, even though all the evidence objectively points to the fact that they are prideful. This person will have trouble saving his or her marriage, until they receive some professional help.

Without the salvation of the mind or how we look at or perceive the world, our character cannot be changed. Very few of us really need clinical help, but many of us, spiritually speaking, from whence we came, need professional help. We really need to sit down, along with our spouses, and talk with an experienced, Christian counselor or even a seasoned Pastor.

We have been exposed to so many things that are hurtful, negative, and life-denying, that our thinking is definitely twisted. One of the conundrums of the human mind and its thinking patterns is that it doesn't know when it's sick and needs help.

Jesus, in His mercy, healed the man without the man overtly asking for healing. When Jesus asked the man about healing, the man gave Him an excuse for why he wasn't healed already.

Likewise, many of us, right now, are experts on our own condition. What we don't know, is how to come out of it. Jesus asked the man to get up and walk. That went against the man's expectation. The man had to show faith in order to be healed in a way that his mind had not conceived.

The Only Voice That Matters

Note that the man also had to attempt to stand up around a pool full of sick people who were all desirous of getting in the water. Only a "fool" would try to stand up without the healing water, when everybody else is desperately trying to get in the water.

My point is that we spend too much time thinking about what "people" are going to say, rather than about our relationship with our spouses being healed. We have our own thoughts about how a situation is going to turn out. Usually, our plan will not work because we are in need of some professional help. There should be no hesitation at all about seeking professional help.

We have to do it God's way. See Illustration 7-1. We all have to know the roles for which we were created. Sometimes we are so far away from those roles, that we need professional help getting back to them.

If the man that Jesus healed had any doubts or reservations about being healed, Jesus would not have been able to heal him. There was help available for him, and there is also help available for you.

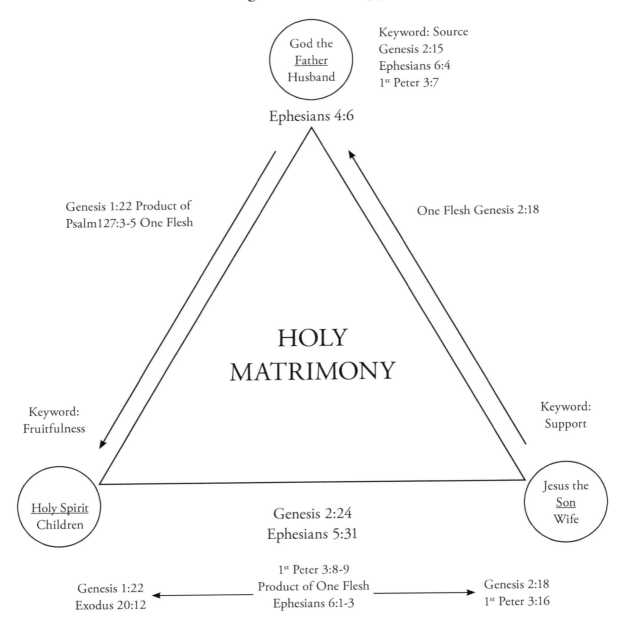

Illustration 7-1
Marriage: A Practical Approach

God the
<u>Father</u>
Husband

Keyword: Source
Genesis 2:15
Ephesians 6:4
1st Peter 3:7

Ephesians 4:6

Genesis 1:22 Product of
Psalm127:3-5 One Flesh

One Flesh Genesis 2:18

HOLY
MATRIMONY

Keyword:
Fruitfulness

Keyword:
Support

<u>Holy Spirit</u>
Children

Jesus the
<u>Son</u>
Wife

Genesis 2:24
Ephesians 5:31

Genesis 1:22
Exodus 20:12

1st Peter 3:8-9
Product of One Flesh
Ephesians 6:1-3

Genesis 2:18
1st Peter 3:16

CASE STUDY – LESSON #7

"PROFESSIONAL HELP"

"Wilt thou be made whole?" John 5:6

Jim and Katie Stringer – "It's Hard!"

In Katie's mind, everything seemed to be happening all at once. The tire blew-out on the way home; the medical test revealed *another* tumor; the neighbors who were no longer "neighborly;" and her daughter, Jill's problems on the job.

It seemed to be too much for Katie – enough to make *anybody* give up. Why does God seem to make life so hard for those who truly believe? Katie Stringer, or "Kate" as she was affectionately called by her husband, was having a bad day to say the least.

She got up that morning late, running as she usually does; putting a load of clothes in the washer and taking the load out of the dryer that she washed last night. She ironed while she was brewing her husband, Jim, a pot of coffee and preparing his morning diet of *"two eggs boiled hard and lightly-browned toast."*

Their granddaughter, Mary Beth, their daughter Jill's only child, had spent the night with them. What a fitful night it was! The little girl tossed and turned all night long – rolling back and forth between Kate and Jim. If it bothered Jim, it didn't show because he snored all night long.

"I guess he is tired," Kate thought, *"he works so hard. Children are definitely meant for the young!"* Kate finished ironing, put the ironing board away, got the paper in, and fed their poodle – Pebbles.

Now it was time to wake Mary Beth and get her something to eat. Kate had another doctor's appointment scheduled for that day along with *another* round of chemo, but she still had to drop Mary Beth off at school *and* go into the office for a half day.

Jim was already up getting ready for his shift at the Mill. He was preparing his own lunch. *"What a sweetheart!"* Kate blew him a quick kiss when she saw he was up, moving around, and trying to help her. Jim gave her a quick, playful tap on the backside as she passed. Before they would leave for the day, they would all gather and pray.

Jim and Kate had established this ritual ever since they were married 30 years ago. Over the years, Jim had been everything that Kate thought he would be and more. She wanted a strong, Christian man, and God sent her one – Jim Stringer. Of course, Kate didn't know it at first, because both she and Jim were the products of unsaved families.

Their parents did attend church every now and then – just like most everyone else in the community. They may have even prayed from time to time, especially before large family meals, like at reunions, on Christmas Day and other festive events.

What their parents didn't do was show any real allegiance to Christ as Savior. While they respected the Bible, they didn't necessarily consider its precepts binding on their lives. The two families – both Jim's and Kate's – were widely and favorably known.

Looking back, Kate could see that people of her parents' generation really only attended church out of habit and tradition. They were good people. They were even "social conservatives": they were *against* abortion, in *favor* of the death penalty, *strongly* against same-sex relationships, and were generally in favor of all things that pertained to family.

Kate realized that both her parents and Jim's merely exhibited the thinking of their generation – it was just a more conservative generation. They didn't have anything original about them – even though they thought they did. They were just another generation of people who were far, far from God.

Kate smiled to herself as she thought, *"the adults of Mary Beth's generation will probably think her parents and Jim's parents were strong Christians who lived in the good old days!"*

Jim and Kate had previously *thought* they were already saved until they were exposed to teaching that the claims made in Scripture are quite real and are binding on all those who would be saved.

Jim, especially, was literally overcome with emotion on his college campus when a student minister, Jim Erskine, quoted a portion of Psalm 100:5 and applied it to Jim. One Jim said to the other, *"Jim, God's truth will endure for all generations."*

Until then, Jim, in his heart of hearts, saw the Bible as almost archaic, an anachronism, a book for generations past but now only for the religious instruction of children, and something that old people – like his parents – liked to read and keep around.

However, Jim Erskine's words struck him deeply. He walked about the campus and attended his classes the next few days in a fog. Was Jesus *really* real? Was salvation a true offer to *him*?

Did God's truth extend to *"all generations"* including the set of highly educated, but morally indifferent people on his campus? Then, too, what about the professors? They, too, were morally indifferent.

They all had their "causes" for which they enlisted students, but none of them seemed overtly religious. In fact, the campus seemed to have a policy of "egalitarianism;" everybody was equal and treated exactly the same: male and female; black and white; rich and poor.

Then, too, there seemed to be such a spirit of idealism amongst all of his friends – they would be the generation to improve the world because they had the latest and the best thoughts about everything – at least that is what they were taught, and that was the spirit on the college campus.

Jim Stringer realized that out of a campus of thousands, if what Jim Erskine said was *really* true, then only a handful of the students were really saved. Those who *were* saved were not popular at all.

Like Jim Erskine, Christian students were generally shunned; they were not well known. They were almost like the blue sky – you didn't notice them unless there was a cloud nearby to add contrast. *"Boy, if other students knew what the Christians really thought, they would be hated instantly. They would be labeled 'judgmental,' and they would be forced to try to prove that what they believe is true,"* Jim thought to himself.

Still Rev. Jim Erskine stayed after Jim Stringer. One day Rev. Erskine told Jim, *"No decision about Christ at all, really is a decision."* Those words pierced Jim's heart, and he was convicted as to the truthfulness of God's Word. Knowing he was about to be ostracized socially, he still submitted to the Gospel message, gave his life to the Lord, and asked Him to live in his heart.

For Kate, it was different. She had graduated from college seven years earlier than Jim, and she was already *"living life,"* while Jim was still in college. In fact, Kate was once engaged to marry Carl, Jill's biological father.

Carl wanted to marry Kate. Who wouldn't want to marry Kate? Kate was beautiful, in an extremely sexy sort of way, but Carl did not want to marry her under those conditions. Against her better judgment, Kate had been living with Carl off and on over the course of three years.

She had a vague notion it was wrong, but there was something about Carl that made co-habitation seem like a step toward marriage. Of course, there was no condemnation from her parents as long as she kept them guessing about her residence and wasn't too open about it.

Then, too, everybody her age was seeing *somebody,* and most of them were living together. If not, then everybody would be lonely. Living together was like a prelude to marriage.

Carl and Kate would fight, and make up, fight and makeup. Sometimes, they would even see other people between the fights, but that was just temporary until they could get back together again.

"*Passion,*" Carl called it. Whatever it was, it seemed to be *really* good at the time. Of course, Carl didn't expect Kate to get pregnant; neither did Kate for that matter. Although she did love Carl, the pregnancy seemed to wake Kate up from a spiritual sleep.

She realized that what she was doing was wrong, but for a different reason from her parents. Her parents would probably want her to stop living with Carl without being married. They would probably be embarrassed since their generation "*just didn't do that.*" Of course, they would be upset about the pregnancy, and insist on marriage out of a sense of duty.

Kate's pregnancy, the baby growing within, gave her some idea of the miracle of creation and childbirth. For the first time in her life, Kate began to have real thoughts about God as He relates to her, *personally.* Then it happened.

On a routine visit to the pre-natal physician's office, Kate was looking at a sonogram of Jill. Then, almost on cue, her doctor began talking about the Son of God – Jesus Christ – who makes "*new life possible.*"

Kate's tears began to flow. She thought about the love Christ must have for her, even as she had love for the still unborn Jill. Kate thought about her recent failures and then other failures from even farther back. As the Holy Spirit convicted her, she began to realize that she was not saved at all. All those years of chasing Carl and other men, were just foolish!

"If God can love me and give Himself for me," she thought, *"then I can live for Him."* Almost, as if reading her thoughts, the doctor quoted Romans 5:8: *"But God commendeth His love toward us, in that, while we were yet sinners, Christ died for us."*

Quietly, but with a determination of spirit, Kate asked the Lord for forgiveness and to live within her. She immediately left Carl whom she could never marry because he was not serious about the Lord or anything else.

Soon Kate would join Smyrna Baptist Church. Smyrna Baptist was a very conservative, Bible teaching and preaching Church. Smyrna seemed to attract those who wanted truth and who desired to live a saved life. Smyrna was small and intimate.

Smyrna was also where Kate would make a profession of faith, be baptized (a second time), and, ultimately, introduced to a new Christian named Jim Stringer. Jim was everything that Kate could have wanted in a Christian man, and was all that she had hoped and prayed for. He accepted Jill as his own child, and they began a journey of faith together so long ago.

From the outside looking in, the years have been tough on Jim and Kate Stringer. Although they have the joy of Christ, they have also been exposed to the anger, persecution, and subtle discrimination that comes along with living in a culture that is inherently *"anti-Christ."*

Jim was passed up for several promotions at the Mill because he did not consider it "career-suicide" to place Christ first. He did not regularly work on Sundays – unless it was an emergency.

He didn't laugh at jokes that were *"off-color"* or hurtful in any way – even though he had told a few himself years ago, when he was much younger and unsaved. Additionally, Jim didn't share in crude and vulgar language. When he heard any, he would just become silent.

Jim was very loving and refused to practice any sort of deceit, backbiting, or subtle cruelty of any kind against others. He knew that he had once done these things, and could easily do these things again, so in his own words, he had to *"keep watch over his heart."*

However, the practice that hurt Jim the most professionally, was that he had to understand, in detail, every new corporate policy so that he could ensure that his conscience was not being violated.

Jim wouldn't sign any document if he didn't know what it meant, and he definitely wouldn't sign it if he knew it was not true. If anyone asked Jim about anything, he would answer truthfully, but lovingly, no matter where he was or with whom he was speaking.

As a result, Jim did not progress very far past entry level. This kept his pay relatively low compared to others, while it also kept him and Kate's living standards very modest. Kate had to carefully manage her paycheck as a time-keeper and Jim's paycheck from the Mill for them to have enough to support their family.

Although the Stringer's only had one child, Jill; Jill proved to be expensive over the years: braces, cheerleader camps, and tutors when the algebra and geometry got too tough for her parents. Of course, there were also the clothes, gowns for senior year, and even a car for graduation. Jill never married, although she was a successful architect in a nearby town.

When she was twenty-five, Jill had a baby out-of-wedlock, Mary Beth. Kate could see it coming a mile away, but she was powerless to stop it. Jill was so enamored with a man on her job. It was almost as if she were watching herself and Carl all over again from a distance. It broke poor Jim's heart.

After being raised in a Christian home, and then all those years of being exposed to good teaching, he just couldn't understand it. Finally, during one of those prayer sessions at the Stringer home, Jill confessed to her mother and father that she was not saved, but she was now truly ready to give her life to the Lord. Gladly and humbly, she submitted to the Gospel message.

The last five years since Jill's conversion have probably been the toughest on the family. Kate was diagnosed with cancer, which brought a disruption to daily routine and an unexpected upheaval in the family budget.

Kate secretly blamed herself for this. She also blamed herself for the effect the chemo was having on the marriage bed. *Jim deserves more of a wife*, she thought.

Jim felt Kate's withdrawal. He assumed it was because of the financial hardship he had brought on the family by not being regularly promoted. Of all people, Jim knew how desperately the family needed finances. Sometimes, he even felt himself to be a failure.

More than once, the great Jim Stringer thought about leaving his family. It all seemed to be too much, and coming at him too fast. He regularly pushed these thoughts out of his mind, but with each new setback, they would return.

Almost at the same time, Jill's conversion brought all kinds of turmoil to her personal life. It was hard living in a large city and being single. She had constant bouts with loneliness resulting in several close calls with "nice guys" from the local church.

Jill was attractive just like her mother; and just like her mother, she loved attention. That is how she ended up with Mary Beth's father – with whom she refused to have any dealings other than those which concerned Mary Beth.

Like Jill suspected when she was younger, she had to suffer in this generation if she would ever really learn how to serve the Lord. She always knew that it would be a struggle; perhaps that is why she never really turned her life over to the Lord, although she was brought up in a Christian home.

She compared herself to Peter before the Crucifixion. She saw the suffering of the truly devoted, and she knew that she, too, had to suffer if she would ever learn to love Him and to follow Him. Jill had devoted herself to her career, which was a very lucrative one. She was able to provide a nice lifestyle for her and Mary Beth, and also help her parents with their medical expenses.

Like her parents years before, Jill knew very few people who claimed allegiance to Christ – although most of her friends were in church. Jill's was a very lonely existence, exacerbated by the fact that she was in another city with no family connection and the constant worry about her parent's finances and her mother's health. Then, too, Jill was faced with a career that was built on a life that, so far, didn't have God at the center.

She wondered many nights whether her parents ever thought about "giving up" when they were younger. She also thought about giving up herself. She needed someone strong in her life – like her step-father.

Would God have her live the rest of her life without any excitement? Would God send her a husband at some point? Why did she have to wait when she was so desperately lonely and so very attractive at the same time?

Then there were thoughts about the job. It definitely provided security, but is it the kind that God wants? She wanted to talk these matters over with her parents, but she didn't want to burden them. *Perhaps*, Jill thought as she dozed off, *I need some professional help.*

QUESTIONS – LESSON #7

"PROFESSIONAL HELP"

"Wilt thou be made whole?" John 5:6

1. Are the pressures that are present in the Stringer home similar to those faced by Christian couples today? If so, name some of those pressures.

_____

_____

_____

_____

_____

2. What are some of the pressures that single, saved Christian parents face?

_____

_____

_____

_____

_____

3. Can a person's thinking change about some things? Why or why not?

_____

_____

_____

_____

_____

4. How has your upbringing influenced your thoughts about marriage and relationships?

_____

_____

_____

_____

_____

5. How has Jill's career both helped and hindered the Stringer family? What do you think she will ultimately have to do, if anything?

_____

_____

_____

_____

_____

6. Do you think the Stringer's did a good job in raising Jill? Why or why not?

_____

_____

_____

_____

_____

7. Is there a generational connection between Kate and Jill? Why or why not?

_____

_____

_____

_____

_____

8. Would it be fair if God allowed Kate to die early and Jill to go through life single? Please explain your thoughts.

_____

_____

_____

_____

_____

9. Does this family need professional help? Why or why not?

_____

_____

_____

_____

_____

10. Why is there such a stigma associated with asking for professional help?

_____

_____

_____

_____

_____

Epilogue

There truly is not one fool-proof "method," or "how-to," on rescuing a marriage. The complexity, diversity, and experience of the parties to a marriage are as varied and manifold as life itself. However, when one understands the origin and purpose of marriage, what was once a bewildering and unfathomable union takes on God's grand design.

The parties to each marriage are at various stages of life experience; hence, what is excellent advice to one couple, may be miserable counsel to another. "Married and Lonely" is presented as a series or distillation of practical, time-tested, and forged-in-fire life lessons.

To master this book is to master each of the lessons, for we all will travel, or have traveled, through each of these lessons. "Married and Lonely" is a good reference guide for life. The lessons that may not be useful now, we will certainly meet later in our lives; whether in our marriages or elsewhere.

Likewise, the lessons that we believe ourselves to have mastered, we will sometimes have to revisit as our circumstances change. After all, what worked at thirty years old, does not necessarily work at sixty-five and beyond!

When you reach the end of "Married and Lonely," you are not actually finished with the book. You have merely had your first experience with concepts and practices that are vital to keeping your life and your marriage healthy.

This will continue to be a life-long challenge, and the book itself will become a valuable resource, as you attempt to avoid being "Married and Lonely."

Lightning Source UK Ltd.
Milton Keynes UK
UKHW052048231219
355900UK00006B/108/P